BOOKS BY *Louis Kronenberger*

◆◇◆◇◆◇◆◇◆

THE CART AND THE HORSE
(1964)

MARLBOROUGH'S DUCHESS
A Study in Worldliness
(1958)

THE REPUBLIC OF LETTERS
(1955)

THE THREAD OF LAUGHTER
(1952)

THE PLEASURE OF THEIR COMPANY
(1946)

KINGS AND DESPERATE MEN
(1942)

These are BORZOI BOOKS, *published in New York
by* ALFRED A. KNOPF

THE CART
AND THE HORSE

The Cart
and
The Horse

BY

Louis Kronenberger

NEW YORK : ALFRED·A·KNOPF

1 9 6 4

AUTHOR'S ACKNOWLEDGMENT

Parts of this book have appeared in *The Reporter, Horizon, What's New, Commentary, The New York Herald Tribune Sunday Magazine, Harper's Bazaar, Mademoiselle, Ramparts, The New York Times Book Review, Vogue, The Texas Quarterly,* and *Encounter.*

L. C. catalog card number: 64–14419

THIS IS A BORZOI BOOK,
PUBLISHED BY ALFRED A. KNOPF, INC.

Manufactured in the United States of America, and distributed by Random House, Inc.
Published simultaneously in Toronto, Canada, by Random House of Canada, Limited.

Published, May 25, 1964
Reprinted, September 1964

TO

W. H. Auden

Contents

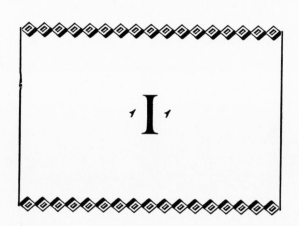

I

OVERTURE
The Cart and the Horse

IT WAS NOT till I had written a number of these essays that I came to see with what they were most concerned, and at whom their comments were chiefly directed. If it was no accident that I had been looking at the more educated and articulate levels of American life, it was still without conscious design. Yet once I saw what I was doing it seemed what I had meant to do. Who of us has not had his say about America's purely "popular" culture, about our sheep-herded, mass-publication-minded living and thinking? And since our mass culture is so scantily a folk culture and so overwhelmingly a fabricated one, not only are our assaults upon it foredoomed, they are also misdirected. When a car goes off the road, we must ask who was driving it. When the ceiling falls in, we must find out what was happening upstairs. Till we focus attention on the taste-makers and pace-setters themselves, we are belaboring people who know not what they do, let alone why they are doing it or what else might be done. Mass culture, nowadays, is never at the crossroads; the basis of superintending it is that it shall never know there *are* any.

Yet, ultimately, it was not with shifting from those who constitute mass culture to those who create it that I was subconsciously concerned. In a way I was no more concerned with the shepherds than the sheep. And where I *was* concerned with the shepherds, it was not really in terms of mass culture—it was with such of them as were forced to be sheep-shearers, or were longing for sheep-folds, or themselves were sheep. But my chief concern was with something else—with a different culture and a different breed. Or, rather, with two differing cultures and breeds, so little harmonized as to be mutually hostile; so far from alike as scarcely to penetrate each other's thoughts; so morally disunited as to be, on the one hand, the most limply complaisant group in America, and on the other the most doctrinaire. The one breed tends to cheapen what they deal with; the other, to deaden it. What these people have in common is nothing that joins them together; only what sets them, as minorities, apart. They are, in very unequal degrees, of superior intelligence, awareness and education; they are, in other words, Americans who in terms of their social, cultural, moral failings should know better.

If this is a very didactic classification, it seems to me a pretty decisive one as well, since it touches a crucial

((4))

nerve, indeed a main artery, of our culture. The real point about these people is that they *should* know better, not that they necessarily do. For some of their short-comings, they can be forthrightly indicted—a willing-ness to succumb to wrong standards and practices; a desire, involving moral laxity, for power or material suc-cess. But though the indictment must stand, there are plainly "extenuating circumstances"—conflicting values, social mandates, economic pressures. In many cases, too, those who should know better may *not* know—whether from faulty perspective, or too limited personal experi-ence; or from neurotically comforting, or even more neurotically harassing, one another; or just from living in an age of very bewildering anxiety, an age that can rob some of them of all fibre, and others of all flexibility.

The great issues of our age are so oppressive, and underlie and overcast so much, that to bring them into this book would make its own procedures unworkable. I can only say, once for all, that my narrowed approach to American culture argues no blindness to vaster forces or more widespread fears. And I can only add that in writing of people who should know better I should doubtless know better myself—should know how often they are victims, or puppets, or end-products, of the harsh forces of our time. But I would hope I do realize this, if only from not seldom feeling victimized also. The problem with us all, surely, is to put in our claims for *final* exculpation while not honoring them as an habi-tual form of excuse.

What seems to me socially, culturally, humanly amiss

in American life as a whole is its way of jumbling its values. The jumbling of values conceivably arises from a reluctance, or even a downright refusal, to formulate any. What with our conformist psychology and deference to public opinion on the one hand, and our susceptibility to sales talks disguised as gospels and to seasonal innovations touted as landmarks of progress on the other, we blinker ourselves against facts, we blind ourselves to all they imply, we regard our sheeplike assent to anything new as proof of our rugged adventurousness. Change, movement, progress—so long as they are material or mechanical—we are always panting to embrace. So great, indeed, is the obloquy in America of being a stick-in-the-mud that, if you just give us new mud, or mud of a new color, or best of all mud under a new high-sounding name, we are the greatest stick-in-the-muds on earth.

Jumbling social and cultural values today is almost the basis of our society and our culture; and though many of the chief motives doubtless apply to bourgeois society in every age, they operate with greater potency, from providing more widespread opportunity, in ours. The pull of vanity, the tug of fashion, the thrust of ambition, the grip of status have not only greatly intensified under twentieth-century bourgeois democracy: its chief *industry* has been to intensify them. The old, orderly curriculum for middle-class advancement—family comfort at 40, prosperous living at 50, community prominence at 60, no longer obtains. It is not just that the ambitious can't wait so long because they probably won't live so

long, but that careers are no longer vertical but circular
—Toledo at 21, Cleveland at 35, Chicago at 48, and in
different corporations as well as cities. Further, in a
publicity-governed culture and a corporation-governed
world, the very rules for advancement have changed.
Once a young man was most esteemed for underplaying
his role, for his modest demeanor—it argued thrift,
sobriety, right thinking. Nowadays he is judged by appearances; and indeed he so judges himself. Formerly
a young couple knew just what possessions they wanted,
what status they aspired to, over the years. But technology has so much become the mother—or the cruel
stepmother—of fashion, that what a young couple
proudly display today may tomorrow be hopelessly dated,
and what they will crave five years hence may not yet
exist.

Consequently—and I mean far beyond man's immemorial talent for self-deception—we have so far
jumbled our values as more and more to reverse their
order and not recognize their make-up. And if we have
put the cart before the horse, it applies not least to those
of us who should know better, who deal in ideas as well
as commodities. Doubtless all bourgeois modes of life
make for certain upside-down values; tend to put ex-
trinsic appeal ahead of intrinsic worth, community
edicts before personal judgments. And certainly in contemporary America fashion goes far beyond clothes and
hair-dos, drinks and diversions. It dominates a whole
cultural outlook—the right suburb, the right street in
the suburb, the right style of house and way of furnishing

it; the right schools and camps and colleges; even concerts and pictures and books.

But there also exist in America less classic reversals.
Thus, thanks to our seeing-eye dogs of advertising and
promotion, we more and more put the packaging ahead
of the product; are fetched by the clever twist, the
snappy slogan, the catchy detail, the glossy surface, the
snooty manner. For one family who heed Consumer's
Report ten hearken to manufacturers' window dressing.
Again, there is much talk about the hard sell, but has it
been stressed what easy marks we are for the hard buy?
The more obstacles to getting into the restaurant, the
more arrogant the headwaiter, the more exorbitant the
price, the more cheek-by-jowl the tables—the greater becomes the incentive to dine there. And similarly with hit
shows, nightclubs, anything that is roped off, that requires pull,* that takes long-term planning; and on a
basis, most of the time, that such popularity isn't de-
served in the least! A docile race even in our frivolities,
we have no instinct for one-upping the one-upsman—
for a better restaurant of our own; but only for reaching
the "right" place ahead of our neighbor. We have to be
among the first to see the Emperor's new clothes.
"Chichi" we murmur of this, or "Brouhaha" of that, all
the time running like hell to see both.

Two other voracious aspects of our bourgeois culture
are its taste for giantism and its craving for status. Just
how far giantism may derive from our early sense of size

* An essay remains to be written on the status value—and
vanity satisfactions—of pull in American life.

about America itself, I do not know; but there seems a more than fortuitous kinship between the tall tale and the tall building, the awareness of untapped resources and the amassing of untold wealth. And the absence, or late growth, or bastard development of civilizing traditions; the lack of understatement in our approaches as well as our humor, must have furthered the rejection of shapeliness for size, and linked expansionist activity with grandiose symbols. Every one in democratic America aspires to a title, and with luck or toil can gain one: Exalted Ruler of a secret society; duty-free vice president of a bank; supernumerary member of a board —something grandiloquent enough to make him, if not an actual success, at least a big-shot nonentity. Size, it may be, has been equally our trump card and our joker. From a primitive ideal, giantism became a human commodity—Chicago's panoramic stockyards, Hollywood's epic imbecilities, Thomas Wolfe's gargantuan tetralogies, the Texas state of mind, the California state of mindlessness.

Our craving for status, which perhaps seems un-American, displays very American traits. Status with us has little in common with foreign traditions of rank: it generally means "Have you arrived?" rather than "Where do you come from?"; or "Do you look right?" rather than "Need you bother to?" However usurious the rates or suicidal the terms, status in America *is* obtainable; the catch is that you cannot achieve it once for all—what you are can put you just as much out of the running as what you used to be. Moreover, status can be as fully attested through being seated at the edge of a dance floor as on the right of a dowager. Keeping up one's end in America almost never allows of playing it down; it is only with a distinct minority that shabby cars or dowdy clothes have their own cachet. If only from being so un-fixed and dynamic, status in a sense has by-passed ordinary snobbery. It comes closer to being in the lead than at the right level; it involves, so to speak, *being there*—if you aren't, it's not that you refused to go but that you weren't invited. Besides, if you're not there, how can you know who else was, or wasn't?

As these comments have tried to show, a great deal in bourgeois American life suffers from being too "real-istic" and hence not realistic at all—from judging, in other words, by what looks right, sounds right, is ac-claimed right; or, from following the crowd so as never to be *disastrously* wrong. Follow the crowd, and even if the stock market crashes, though you may be painfully out of pocket, you will not be out of step. Compared to those a generation ago, today's formulas for living are more urbane, its mandates for success less crudely philistine; but the directives, *as* directives, are not less scrupulously followed, either as the right way to play the game or the only way to beat it.

In a sense, what Poor Richard counseled on a hard-headed, prudential eighteenth-century basis, nineteenth-century America elevated into a form of idealism. And in the twentieth century much of this has simply been warmed up and served with *sauce diable*, adding a pinch of mockery to its recipe for the main chance. Americans are uneasy when there isn't a strong element of horse sense in their approach to living, but they feel a little uneasy, too, if there is no suggestion of the higher life. What they seek is a down-to-earth guide book with a page from the prayer book for preface—which may help explain why they have become so inventive a nation, whether of self-helpful gimmicks to enhance security, or of gospels involving bran or cold baths that make salvation arduous but wonderfully specific. All this, in the end, makes for a realistic approach that is actually a flight from reality; for a reliance on facts in every sense except that of facing them.

American life, one might add as a footnote, is often on the wrong road, and even moving in the wrong direction, from its credulousness about road signs. Many misleading ones have been, from far back, of the Devil's conniving; or of the gentlemen who preside over Wall Street panics, or chop up "national" issues, or mince the news, or spice the lies. Moreover, the signposts seem unimpeachable in view of what high ground they seem to point to, and of what splendid monuments men have caused to rise there—museums and universities, churches and hospitals, laboratories and libraries:

> *Come raise a glass to Leland Stanford,*
> *To Hill and Frick and Rockefeller:*
> *Their names are now genteel as* Cranford,
> *Their place just this side Helen Keller.*
> *Seemly as music for the organ*

THE CART AND THE HORSE

The libraries Carnegie reared
(Or Huntington, or J. P. Morgan):
Those most reviled end most revered.

The road signs have been so misleading, of course, because they were afterthoughts. The Devil's disciples never, themselves, paid the slightest heed to road signs —or traffic lights. Theirs was a true realism and, to die in an odor of sanctity, they put the buccaneering before the benefactions, the dung before the horse.

· 2 ·

So much for our pursuit of the Main Chance, for our middle-class conditioning. What, as I wrote this book, most disturbed me was the extent to which those who, from knowing better, should help lead the rest of America out of the wilderness, themselves seemed headed for it, themselves were jumbling values. They too, however great their intelligence or concern with ideas, seem often swayed by slogans; have too often aped fashion, eyed status, exalted size; been conformist —and careerist as well. They frequently did more than follow the signposts; they erected them. They it was who at one level minced the news, or at a higher one dried out the classics; prostituted art or emasculated it; and made name and thing as antithetical as spirit and letter.

The business of packaging-before-product has come to loom so large, for itself being today's parent American

((12))

product, whether as advertising, promotion or salesmanship. And right here a superior breed, right here people who should know better, are the very poets of packaging and psychologists of surface lure—are tirelessly applying the business principle that a thousand commercial billboards can crystallize into a cultural inscription; that a thousand house-organ manifestos can add up to an intellectual belief. For mass audiences the major theme may be glossiness or snob appeal; but for other audiences there are other approaches, so that even the Man from Missouri proves no match for the boy wonder in New York. Let me be the first to cry *touché*. Needing, in Seattle, an old-fashioned gargle for sore tonsils, I visited two austere "Prescription Expert" pharmacies, and one very solemn "Dispensing Chemist," to find all three ignorant of the remedy, all three bored at the very thought of anything so low-priced, all three hurriedly pushing toward me "the best thing around"—wherefor I came away with two luxury mouthwashes and a cough lozenge. Had I been less impressed by the dedicated look of the dispensaries, and by their stately nomenclature, I might easily have found my gargle at any cut-rate drugstore; as it was, having crossed the frontier, I got it in Vancouver for 40¢.

The austerity come-on, the Clinical Look, the Scholarly Aura, is the counter gimmick of an age whose chief one is glossiness. Here the absence of packaging is the great trick of packaging; in an era of high style and Beautyrest, anything monastic or downright uncomfortable signifies unflawed integrity. Since all this demands an adequate terminology, Dickens's Circumlocution Office has, with somewhat altered aims, reopened on Madison Avenue. For every "mortician" laughed out of existence, a dozen "corrective posture consultants" and "investment-portfolio counselors" are firmly entrenched; for one "halitosis" (that piled up a fortune even while becoming a joke), a dozen commercialized polysyllables exude laboratory selflessness and lifetime research. In the arts, there is austere packaging too—the jargon by which professors indoctrinate their students, pedagogues explicate their texts; there is even an annex to the Circumlocution Office, a thriving *Boutique des Clichés Supérieurs*. All these various packagings—the rich-in-butterfat sleeping pill, the reversible—i.e., silk-lined—hair shirt, the teeth-straightening gumdrop, the shock-treatment stall shower, the Unabridged Moby-Dictionary, flourish and propagate, regardless of whether the therapy works or the commentary sheds light.

Status, the inner spring of our vast Organizational Society, looms large with our educated classes as well, whether with our mouthpiece professions at one end or our academics at the other. And just because what our mouthpieces, our advertising and promotion corps, purvey become status symbols with the public at large, the purveyors, having so big a stake in the transaction, must campaign for themselves while conscripting others. With them, the job itself is the occupational hazard. The vulgarity involved in their making a living in time pervades their life. The timorous ruthlessness that characterizes their professions breeds the self-pitying cynicism that furthers their careers. Their need for status means displaying every shred of it they already have; means living in glass houses with all the lights on; means being a walking scrapbook, and a whispering scandal sheet to boot. Compared to ordinary lives of quiet desperation, these people are part of a dressy Reign of Terror. And what they are part of is indeed a form of social revolution. Where, for example, parents once struggled to achieve the right neighborhood and house, the right school and dancing school, with their children's future in mind, analogous efforts today have in mind the parent's immediate standing. The muffled social campaign is now a steam-calliope onslaught.

Meanwhile, the concern for status has rubbed off on more "serious" or "sensitive" people, if only because they themselves rub shoulders at times with the careerists. The exalted status that *ambivalence* enjoys as a concept in intellectual circles may be ironically, or quite realistically, reflected in how many highbrows now occupy ambivalent positions—run with the hares and hunt with the hounds, write for all kinds of media, have TV reputations, compete among themselves for lucrative posts. Status, again, helps condition their price for articles, their fees for lecturing, their desire for honors. The fact that this is an achieved aspect of our culture only makes more difficult the criteria by which they must regulate their conduct—must judge how far their "knowing better" is a cultural obligation, and how far it is a career liability. The ambivalent position can extend to academic life; but even where it doesn't, the academic struggle for status has classically bred a pedagogical self-importance, a hierarchic campus society, a "full professor" frame of mind, a mingled scorn and envy of the outside world.

Giantism, too, has distorted the thinking of those who should know better, and not just of those who purvey it, with their commitment to big-shot psychology. Giantism has infected the very people who protest the bourgeois forms of it—I mean, once again, the intellectual and academic world. "Significance," or some form of symbolic size, is so preeminent an academic yardstick, and minute analysis so preeminent a critical method, that only "major" works have any standing. Literature today goes by bulk, by weight—top weight is the one-man show, the full-semester seminar in Melville or Yeats. But those underweight—say, Scott Fitzgerald—can be fattened up, like Strasburg geese, to qualify. A Cyclopean, or one-eyed, giantism pervades Academe scarcely less—all Jane Austen and no Trollope; all *The Ambassadors* and no *The Egoist;* all Pascal and no La Rochefoucauld. We deplore the huge disparity between the sales of best-sellers and bookclub choices on the one hand, and of all the rest of current publications on the other. But what of the vast academic imbalance between certain classroom "musts" and all the rest of established literature? It would be well worth knowing the annual college sales of Robert Frost as against Edwin Arlington Robinson, of *The Great Gatsby* as against *A Passage to India,* even of *Huck Finn* as against *Life on the Missis-sippi.* Here the figure of giantism exhibits the face of conformity; the effect is so standardized as to convey a sense of academic chain stores.

Indeed, today's greatest jumbling of *serious* values involves the opposition between education and culture. If I make opposites of what seem natural allies, it is to give names to two ultimately conflicting desiderata, two quite distinct climates in contemporary life. Certain differences that will seem plain are not wholly to my present purposes. Thus, many would think it wrong for education to take precedence of culture on the very ground that it must necessarily precede it. No one would maintain that education is, like culture, an *end;* when it becomes one, as for the scholar, we call it learning. Again, for individual accomplishment, or professional career, education is indispensable where culture is not —wherefore, we see that while education involves something utilitarian, culture implies something disinterested. An "educated" community suggests standards about housing, living conditions, schools, playgrounds, hospitals and the like; but its residents can as easily be insurance salesmen as scientists, bridge-players as concert-lovers. A cultivated community, on the other hand, suggests a way of life rather than just standards of living.

My setting education against culture, and deploring that it has been raised so high above it, rests on less familiar distinctions—distinctions that, though widely applicable, are by comparison far more restrictive. By the educated, I mean here the truly, unequivocally educated, not brokers who went to college; I mean people whose approaches are no less intellectual than informed, not bright boys who become TV announcers. I mean superior people, whether in intellect, scholarship or *expertise;* aware, often learned people, not just knowledgeable in one field. By culture I mean a number of things harmoniously interfused—reach of mind, plasticity of feeling, urbanity of approach, a sensitive responsiveness to art, a strong concern for humanistic values. As I have remarked elsewhere, education means light—glare and all; culture, the shaded bulb; not glare but glow. Educated people do indeed speak the same languages; cultivated ones need often not speak at all.

Now, since the education that I find over-exalted is in its kind of a very high sort, not surprisingly it will rest on Higher Education itself—whether those who inculcate it and form others in their own image or those whom they equip for the outside world. We may call the first group academics; the second, intellectuals. For illustration, let me use the field I know best, the field too with the widest spread for culture—literature. Here as elsewhere, the vast accretion of knowledge in modern times, and the staggering result in research, has made for whole granaries, even whole department stores, of fact and theory, materials and meanings. And along with all the new gospels—psychiatric, anthropological, sociological, epistemological, mythopoeic—there are all the new gadgets: tape-recordings, microfilm, X-rayed MSS, writers' "papers" in university libraries. Every novelist's jottings, today, can make for a reversal of judgment, every poet's doodles can help explain his art. Something has to be done with it all; and near every granary or gravel-pit is built a graduate school. Thus far no harm is done. Confined to the graduate schools, the assorted data can produce things of real value, while simultaneously creating a kind of crank culture, a series of communities where men lead a buried life unearthing the buried life of others, or find meaning in life for themselves through trying to find meanings beyond the usual meanings in other people's. Given decent incomes and docile wives, they could have a high old time fraternizing and talking shop with the aid of marginal scrawls and variant spellings, frayed postcards and faded ink. Unfortunately, the work done in graduate schools doesn't remain inside their walls. Nor do the workers. The graduate students *in turn* become teachers; they write; they edit; they co-edit; they General-Edit; and theirs are no heavy tomes chained to lecterns, but required textbooks, compulsory source books, indispensable "surveys." They grow old, they grow old, they see 471 students enrolled. Of these, 49 will presently enter the Graduate School. The 422 others, reading five texts during a period of four months, will at length go forth to become bond salesmen, skin surgeons, commission merchants, airline executives—knowing more about *King Lear, Faust, The Red and the Black, The Wings of the Dove* and *The Idiot* than the most cultivated men-of-letters. True, they may not know who wrote *Wilhelm Meister* or *The Eternal Husband,* nor have ever seen a canvas of Caravaggio's or heard a note of Bellini. But of their Five-Inch Shelf they will be past masters.

Meanwhile, having moved from the campus out into the world, a whole corps of intellectuals are exerting upon literature a very miscellaneous equipment, an ambidextrous surgical skill. Theirs is no commerce with jottings and doodles and line-by-line readings. For them, all the new "disciplines" crowd and caress one another; theirs the study of what the psychiatrist can bring to a masterpiece, and the anthropologist find in it, and the sociologist take away. The artist's divided nature, the dark condition of man—these they set forth to reveal, wearing miners' lamps in their forehead, bearing surgeons' scalpels in their hands, rooting out human maladies, social malignancies, religious epilepsies, psychiatric protuberances. That literature should be a vast open port is clearly salutary. That a work of art must have truth of perception under it, the light of understanding behind it, and inside it some sense of personal or racial memory, we are all agreed. And as our knowledge of art—and of the creative process itself—has deepened; as science, in wrestling with chaos, has augmented complexity, necessarily the approach to literature has altered, the keys to comprehension have multiplied, and what they unlock has revealed new secret drawers in turn. We can no more judge literature through Matthew Arnold's eyes than could he through Dr. Johnson's. But we can still, I would think, approach it in the broad humanistic spirit that they did. Yet where literature today is not being turned into a buried city it flourishes as a bustling trading post. The two attitudes constitute extremes. With neither attitude is literature a full-bodied vintage wine;

((20))

on the one hand it is a mixed drink heavy with sediment; on the other, a religious libation subjected to chemical analysis.

Shorn of excesses, both schools have value: the one stresses the esthetic experience, the other the cultural framework. At the right and left of a central humanist position, they could be notable minority voices, brilliantly lopsided schools of thought. But, if only by colliding, they coalesce today into center as well as sides. Perhaps the Libationists do less harm, for their concern *is* with literature, and one can profit by their discoveries while rejecting their dogmas. With the Sediment School you sometimes feel that the book in question has come to them for a check-up. By the time they are through, they have pounded it and punched it, stethescoped and cardiogrammed, taken X-rays and blood counts. The book doesn't exactly die of its symptoms: it merely becomes the sum of them.

A particular curse with both schools is the kind of recruits they gain. Those of the first school love rules and regulations and pore over their manual of arms; those of the second love rifle practice and gunfire and bang away on the cultural range. Were it not for their virtuous sense of joining the colors and serving the cause, they might both be ignored. But as self-righteous battalions mowing down the deeper values of a civilization they think they defend, they cannot be ignored. It is not just how many qualities in art—elegance, shapeliness, spontaneity, urbanity, worldly insight—they themselves ignore, but how much in any sensitive response to literature they alter or outlaw, how indeed responsiveness goes begging, with analysis enthroned. Often, moreover, how convincing characters or scenes may be is quite secondary to how symbolic or complex.

Complexity has become a chief criterion of depth, anxiety a primary ingredient of art. Indeed, where some ages have suffered from a too smug sense of assurance, ours has perhaps begun to suffer from too grandiose a sense of dislocation. Nor is this a sound matter of rejecting facile cures, but rather one of courting only *sinister* ailments. Evil, in Dostoevsky or Melville or Faulkner, somehow flatters us; ill nature merely belittles. Intellectualist criticism cares nothing for the intercepted glance as against the guilt-ridden gaze, or for mere dry cleaning as against purification. And the damned, to be sure, are far more fascinating than the soup-stained. But in life many are soup-stained and few are damned; and from the intercepted glance a veteran knowledge of life can infer volumes. Such knowledge tots up the cost—to the philosopher no less than the philistine—of vanity, anger, fatuousness, envy, pique. It grasps, no matter how much a sudden aperçu can startle, how pitilessly a home truth can sting. And it recalls that most really great writers have been quite as accurate with the tape measure as with the plumb line.

The misfortune is that the buried-city and the trading-post states of mind not just rule their own worlds but invade undergraduate classrooms and whole areas of criticism. What, ten years later, will an intelligent, responsive chemist or engineer retain of a close reading of

The Wings of the Dove except how it was taught? How different for him is the "discipline" of literature than for the literary-minded the vaunted "discipline" of geometry? Professors, to be sure, have grown canny in their methods. One of their chief current clichés is that literature must be enjoyed, must give pleasure. Not least wonderful is the need to convert the thought into an injunction; and no doubt the pious do put their minds to it, do work away at it, and in time exultantly exclaim: "I can read with pleasure now!" much as a child should cry out: "I can swim now! Watch!"

The obligation to make literature truly rewarding to a large intelligent class is not to deny the existence of a natural élite whose concern for art is far more instinctive and exacting. But there can hardly be greater delusions of grandeur than to suppose that, by approving the principle of an élite, you automatically become a member of it. We must sharply distinguish between membership in an élite in terms of high culture, and the self-propagation of eunuchs in terms of the Graduate Schools. Now many excellent men teach in graduate schools, and many excellent students enroll there. But each group, in both attitude and ability, form a minority. Far too often those who teach have no literary gifts, nor even an inborn naturally sensitive feeling for literature; while just as often those who are taught show few symptoms of either. Doubtless, from its blatant excesses and idiocies, the Graduate School is taking an unfair beating today. But even attacks on it would seem to ignore more central reasons for attack. Let me mention an article by

Mr. Louis D. Rudin Jr.—"What's Wrong With Graduate
Literary Study?" Mr. Rudin tells of a young man who at
23 came to Hollins College for his M.A.:

> He read Proust, Joyce, Faulkner, Yeats, Eliot;
> he studied intensively in the forms of literary
> criticism, he was tutored in Shakespeare, literary
> archetypes, Milton. He had a wonderful time, and
> he was confirmed in his ambition to pursue lit-
> erary study as a career.

"To do that, however," Mr. Rudin continues, "he needed
a Ph.D." Hence Mr. R— H— enrolled at an important
graduate school, where his first assignment was a course
in bibliography. He was taught, as a matter of fact, to
recognize "variant printings of the letter 'P' in Dickens'
Pickwick Papers, so as to tell one edition of that work
from another."

And Mr. Rudin very cogently goes on to document
and denounce the absurd Graduate-School stupidities
practised in the name of "discipline" and "scholarship."
Moreover, the appalling extent to which these practices
flourish constitutes not just a strong indictment of prevailing values; it is clearly a strong indication of pedagogical vested interests. All the same, what Mr. R— H—
was doing—at a much higher level—at Hollins is worth
thinking about too. First of all he was studying just those
writers who are academically *de rigueur* today; was involved in a conformism, a fashionableness, a procedure
Procrusted with dogmas. Furthermore, one gets the
sense that he was for the first time really coming to grips

with Proust, Joyce, Yeats & Co. at the age of 23! In the frivolous 1920s, any one at all seriously literary-minded, any one worth his salt, would have gone at their equivalents—and even at most of *them*—by himself at 19 or 20. And if I'm wrong, and Mr. R— H— had himself earlier discovered and devoured Proust, Joyce and the rest, then —though I quite acknowledge the need of a more systematic study of them—might he not, at 23, have been encouraged to "read" other writers, less fashionable and fore-ordained?

The answer, I fear, is that except in rare instances he could not have been. I know nothing in middlebrow, or even in middle-class, circles that equals the conformity of many members of English departments; this fact alone is enough to invalidate their claims to membership in an élite. For the true members of any élite are always stirring up the waters, always reappraising fashionable names, always finding new or neglected ones to bring forward. What we most look for in a critic is clarity and sharpness of vision; but, failing that, is a kind of rewarding, uniquely revealing astigmatism. But this is precisely what academic teaching won't tolerate. This is what makes most academics highbrow by identification rather than identity. The natural highbrow is always something of a lone wolf, happily on the prowl for discoveries, for provender of his own—wondering what Mungo Park is like, or how Kingsley would read today, or whether Le-Fanu wrote really good novels, or Hebbel good plays, or Sarcey good criticism. Like all true travelers, whether among cities or books, he is not sightseer but rambler, fearless of slums, favorable to honky-tonks, with a passion for period architecture and a weakness for graveyards.

With the *symbol* of education so greatly stressed at both ends of American life—with the B.A. a tollgate to a business career, the Ph.D. to an academic one—we are making education itself an arbitrary equivalent of ability. In the field of teaching, the very situation can be grim enough; but it is made needlessly grimmer. The relatively low pay that follows a long, often hard-to-finance preparation is a dispiriting matter. So is the slow advancement; and in many cases, advancement from assistant to associate professor is not a step but a watershed; involves not just higher salary and title, but tenure; can mean—for reasons that do not reflect on the teacher—being either promoted or dropped. All this is hazardous enough, but it is further complicated by an often irrelevant hazard, by that touchstone for academic promotion—the publishing of books. Sometimes the books will indeed be the professor's best claim to promotion, the best proof of his ability or learning. But often they may prove his poorest claim; and just so, they make us ask: How much has writing books to do with a man's classroom ability and effectiveness?

It seems to me obvious that there are three valuable kinds of professors: those with teaching gifts, those with scholarly gifts, those with critical ones. No doubt the really superior teacher will qualify on more heads than one. But, assuming no real deficiency of background or defectiveness of judgment, a man who can truly teach, who can infuse something vigorous and memorable into his manner, who can inspire something responsive and thoughtful in his students, is surely the type most valuable in the classroom itself. Yet this man may have no talent for writing and nothing very momentous to say. But when I asked of a superior professor why the born teacher, the proved teacher, must keep on turning out books—in most cases, mediocre ones—he broke in on me with: "No, no! They *have* to write—otherwise they get sloppy." I'm afraid I must wonder why. I must wonder whether, grinding out books they have neither talent nor taste for, they won't be as much drained by the effort as misrepresented by the result; whether *writing* books won't make them sloppy, or at any rate won't use up energies far better expended in class. Surely such men stand exactly opposite to many university scholars, who are not effective in the classroom but whose books do communicate much of value to fellow-scholars and to students beyond their own campuses. Isn't a real on-campus value as legitimate as a beyond-campus one?

It is of course the third type of professor, the one with critical gifts, who dominates the academic scene today; and for him, writing books is the natural outlet of his talent, and is indispensable to his career. He deserves his prominence, but as a type he is in some ways causing mischief. For one thing, through gaining most of the campus plums and the beyond-campus prestige, he is the model for all kinds of young aspirants. For another thing, through growing particularly authoritarian in manner, he is often setting dogmatism above free inquiry. Finally, when we drop below the very distinguished top level of critic-teachers—and these cannot be too highly praised—we soon encounter every manner and level of critical books. There are enough good books among them to permit the mere born teacher not to add books of his own; and enough bad ones to encourage him not to. And if the born teacher is denied advancement from his failure to write, there is something very shortsighted about it. Undergraduate students desperately need vibrant teachers—and I don't mean "personalities" or showmen—who can communicate the full far-reaching sense of literature no less than the meanings of particular books. The born teacher is a real *voice*, something surely as good as men who are erudite echoes. Not that undergraduates always realize this: they are so conditioned today as to be mad for "meaning" and "sources" and "symbols." Thus, when I teach Shaw's plays, there are always students who want to write term papers on Creative Evolution: here they have plenty of meaning to wrestle with, plenty of sources to track down and theories to enunciate—and no true connection with literature whatever.

Teaching standards have certainly risen in the colleges, but teaching perspectives have shrunk. If we have, on the one hand, the career-conscious student for whom degrees have a cash value, on the other we have the academic-minded professor whose concerns are too much the counters of his own special world. He cannot form taste without freezing it, expound things without "placing" them, nor does he seem to realize that you can everlastingly impose the best and get nowhere unless you arouse a real desire for it and permit an ultimate search, a personal decision. For though a man's taste is subject to scrutiny, his temperament lies beyond it. I remember Newton Arvin looking up from a book of Allen Tate's essays and saying: "Thank God, *he* doesn't like Stendhal either!" Now Stendhal is my favorite novelist, but as much, I suspect, for temperamental reasons as critical ones; and that two excellent critics should have, on the same basis, a totally different reaction to mine proclaims both the humanity of letters and the sanctity of selfhood. For myself, I must wonder at people who show no blind spots; I must think that a man's lack of temperament *is* subject to scrutiny. Surely equal esteem for, say, Proust and Melville is a little strange.

What is not strange is that bright students with their own emerging idiom of thought are bored today with much that they do, to the point, even, of quitting college. I wonder whether some new kind of degree isn't conceivable, one that would in no way replace the B.A. or dispute its virtues. Call it an Auditor's Degree: the student would neither take examinations nor write traditional term papers, but be charged with a certain amount of writing inspired, however marginally, by the subject-matter of the course. This would not be easier than exams or term papers; would offer no aid and comfort to snap-course addicts or dilettantish playboys—it might well be more demanding. Adolescent poses, nose-thumbing defiances, pretentious nonsense would be scored off; but ungrammatical pungency of style, brilliant wrong-

headedness of argument, well-defended unfashionable-
ness of taste would win points. A true basis would exist
for growth without conventional measuring-rods, and
for self-development to attempt its own self-discipline.

I make the suggestion in a quite realistic spirit, because I think there are those for whom it might work.
But I make it even more from a sense of its symbolic
value, from a feeling that there should be available to the
inquiring, free-spirited young a chance for growth that
stresses personal response, that honors temperament,
that sees the college period as one of protected trial-and-
error; and not so much a "preparation" for life as a pres-
entation of the enrichment life has to offer. At any rate,
it is not how much, on graduating, a man knows, but
how much he cares—and cares for something better,
even, than knowledge. If I am driven here into clichés of
a sort, it is because they seem the only useful cultural
commandments. For, despite all the baccelaureate fine
phrases, education in this country is formalized: in realistic practice it ends the day a man leaves his last classroom. The only true exceptions to this are those who
further pursue it for professional reasons, and those who
are essentially self-educating, for whom art and thought
and knowledge are meat and drink. Otherwise, post-
college living, with its economic pressures, its social demands, its fatigue-spotted leisure, leaves men's "background" to tarnish, or makes any talent they possess into
a "tool." Education today is not just too overt, specific,
up-to-date to create something both civilized and civilizing; it is too career-minded, too winner-directed, to make

for anything so disinterested. Whether, as auditor's degree or anything else, a *modus operandi* can exist for neither losing the whole world nor losing one's own soul, I am far from knowing. But we surely need something workable in American life—which, just so, will not be too strictly ordered, or big-dimensioned, or aggressively intellectual—that will culturally constitute "a number of things harmoniously interfused." The word *civilized* has a little lost caste, but it ought not to be sniffed at, or linked with phrases like *gracious living*. Nor, for what I mean here, does it extend quite far enough. But surely we are setting education above something that frowns on certain bad offshoots of education—that would outlaw what is contentious, over-competitive, authoritarian, self-important. Culture, so regarded, is something, again, that if it cannot change human nature, can modify social conduct; that, if no assurance of deep or original thought, does sharpen perceptiveness, values, taste. It is not perfection; it won't bring us to Elysium. But it could produce men of many different kinds, a whole race of men, who at 40 or 50 bear out the human promise, retain the enlightened perspectives, care for the distinguished pleasures, of their college years. It is not Elysium; but for precisely that reason it need not be Utopia, either.

From Main Street *to* Madison Avenue

SINCLAIR LEWIS is out of fashion, and it may be for not wearing well artistically; but surely it is also because his books are out-of-date. The two most famous of them once pressed their titles into the language: Main Street, through Lewis, came to symbolize what was most repressive and parochial in small-town life; and Babbitt still stands for a type not readily described by any name but his own. But it is a type we today are not so often given to describe: it still abundantly exists but it also, thanks to Lewis, became aware of itself and in some sense altered itself. If it never quite changed its spots, it did at times change its blind spots, it veneered certain prejudices, revised certain perspectives. A generation after *Babbitt*, Babbitt, rather than sniffing at a trip to Europe, had much oftener gone there; and dining out, did not always order steak or roast beef; and dining at home, looked neither fearful nor fretful at something unprecedented in a casserole; and wheresoever dining, did not always talk only shop or sport. He undoubtedly played golf, but sometimes in summer tagged after his wife into antique shops; he certainly played cards, but by way of crossword puzzles had ascended to word games; and if he laughed at Greenwich Village, there was better reason to laugh at it now, and better people laughed with him. If he was a bore, there he conceivably surpassed his earlier self, knowing by now so much more to be boring about.

In any case, by now he had become thematically a bore, and to those most likely to scrutinize him, he no longer had topical interest or much more than historical value. The sociologist had moved on to something else, the satirist to something different. Beyond what a Depression and a New Deal and a World War had brought about, life had itself subtly altered, Babbitt had grown a little more like other people and other people, perhaps, a little more like him. With the passing of time, the great Schools of Business had more and more brought the sales chart and the college diploma under one roof. Thanks to Education, with its new nickname Technology, Babbitt over the years had been split two for one, into the Outer Directed Man and the Other Directed Man. Kiwanis had a country-club look, Philistia wore Suburbia's tweeds, the faces at the businessmen's outing reappeared at the college reunion: horizons have perhaps not drastically widened, but areas have been decidedly enlarged. Consciously or not, two former enemies have shown a willingness to meet each other halfway. As Babbitt started up the stairs, Culture started down, and if the two have not yet met, they are within hailing distance of each other and will any day swap pleasantries on the landing. For where Babbittry seemed confined to the world of business, the long arm of Conformity now embraces a much wider world of culture.

The new conformity, or standardization, has not only altered the Babbitt-that-was; it has also altered the Main Street-that-was, by making it parochial on a nationwide basis. What was once so oppressive, so obstructive, so hopeless about Main Street was in a way what was most forgivable about it. It was small-town in an immemorial sense, wholly lacking in awareness and breadth, as indifferent to the outside world as it was all snoop and pry within. Even its gossip needed nothing very succulent to feed on: an old maid's yearning for the minister, a young man's craving for the bottle, Mrs. Wilson's letting the cake burn for her card party—these enriched the community life quite as much as did bigamy and embezzlement in more enlightened centers. And if small-town life was arid and stifling, on just that account it forced any one with a sense of wider horizons to break away; indeed it came to symbolize revolt as well as repression. And Main Street, forty years ago, had in spite of Sinclair Lewis a certain real character and charm. Ultimately the life of all small towns might show the same crippling limitations, but each had its own seductive touches of local color, if only the levee or the bandstand in the park. And how much each town might have to lose in terms of such things is borne out today when it often has nothing to lose but its chain stores.

Main Street's virtues are in other words tending to vanish, while its vices persist. The small-town mind, the small-town petty interests remain, but what had been a parochial teaspooning of conformism has given way to a nationwide ladling of it. This has, of course, its real advantages, all the mechanized ones that bring greater ease and convenience to life. And to be fair, if standardization helps efface individualism, it also tends to reduce inequality and—thanks to the gadgets by which life is standardized—to amplify leisure. And technology has bridged all sorts of gaps, whether between rich and poor, or city and country, or youth and age. Thanks to TV, the mountains now come to Main Street; and if they won't, thanks then to a plane, Main Street in a trice can go to the mountains.

But standardization, in terms of time-saving devices, has universal endorsement. It is only where it makes for time-wasting proclivities that protest enters in. For the added leisure of small-town life has in general become wholly standardized leisure. After dinner, on goes the dishwasher; then, ten seconds later, the TV. And thanks to such teamwork, Main Street's taste for gossip, or interest in sex, has grown far more cosmopolitan. In fact, that demolition of privacy which is perhaps TV's supreme gift to the nation, now titillates with its innuendos, and enchants with its inquiries, and instructs with its responses, all those who once happily wiped the dishes thinking of Marge Wilson's burnt cake.

((35))

But that a headier brand of gossip now circulates through Gopher Prairie is less menacing in itself than for what it has displaced. The sad thing is that with the coming of TV one real virtue of small-town life has surely diminished—the necessary dependence at times on inner resources; the being alone with one's self or one's reveries or thoughts; the daily portion of brooding time. A man whittling a stick was not always really idle, a woman crocheting a scarf was not just manually employed. To be sure, brooding time could mean brooding over one's resentments, and was never assurance of bona-fide thought. But this new kind of life that saves people so much time has few good pointers on how then to spend it, and has certainly depleted the old stock of small-town wisdom—something that made up for intellectual intolerance with considerable human insight.

Still, Main Street—however instructive the symbol, or confining the reality—has never been part of the Main *stream* of American life, from being, in that precise metaphorical sense, so tributary to it. It has *fed* the main stream: for any one with dreams or ambitions or talents, whether a Horatio Alger character or a Sherwood Anderson one, the small town has been the place to get out of—a fateful exit, a first-act curtain. It provided roots; often—on condition they be transplanted—very rewarding ones. But it is only after the second-act curtain goes up, to reveal our hero now under college elms or city lights or corporation scrutiny, that he becomes part of the great American drama. And in 1964, when he is conceivably the college or office mate of Babbitt's grandson, he will be associated with a great variety of other young people, who bear famous names, or foreign ones, or changed ones; who look friendly or over-friendly, ill-adjusted or too well adjusted—or who just look, wearing an expression that itself is worth a look. Here are young people on the point of entering businesses and professions, and becoming types. The types themselves may, as it were, be movable types, sometimes moving no more than a button up or down, or substituting vodka for gin, or charcoal for grey flannel; but sometimes, too, opening a long-shut social door, or rounding a long-shunned social point. And these movable types are in general moving upward, on those same stairs that Babbitt started up; and Culture, if it starts a bit higher now, still keeps moving down. The landing where they meet has in fact become one of the most significant levels in our contemporary life, and its precise location—which is to say, how few or many steps up for the young man, and how few or many down for Culture—is the clue to how salubrious a level we now live at.

For ours is a much changed world from Babbitt's. It has changed under our very noses, through such striking phenomena as TV and Exurbia and air travel; and has become not just a world of nuclear physics, but one actually of space men and government grants to get to the moon. In a sense, however, man on the moon will still seem remote even if proved real—or at least as against man on the office treadmill or the corporation ladder or the corporation carpet; and if Jules Verne is old hat, Lewis's portrait of Babbitt is almost a daguerrotype. Even the pose is out-of-date: what Lewis showed Babbitt either facing away from or uneasily facing up to, he now turns smilingly toward. He now, as I have said, moves briskly up toward the landing—having taken his first faltering steps thither during the 20s, when a college degree had become a real business advantage as well as a social necessity. But for the Babbitts, during the '20s, culture still *stopped* with college; there were no further supplies of it, and twenty years after graduating they might retain little more than blurred memories of the racier parts of *Tom Jones* or the incompleter Greek statues. Sometimes these memories were eked out with fresher ones obtained in Europe, for Europe was now a reputable place to visit. It was still, especially with Prohibition in force at home, a continent of *Nachtkultur,* of the vibrant night life of Harry's Bar and the Folies Bergère, of a squint at the demi-monde and a snort at the Dome. Still, Babbitt's womenfolk sometimes dragged him to the Louvre or the Uffizi or St. Peter's, and he could still remember what the guide had said about a picture, though sometimes not which picture it was.

And, time passing, Babbitt found that his son didn't want to go into the family carpet business; but by now, when his son favored architecture, Babbitt wasn't likely to get upset. As a matter of fact, where ten years earlier a "modern" house was something for Babbitt to hoot at, in ten years more it would be something he might even want to build. And, more time passing, Babbitt's world acquired more windows—indeed, great wide picture windows—to look out of, upon a more spacious and, indeed, more picturesque world. He discovered too that Art had its forms, its sometimes tax-deductible forms, of horse racing; and so in a small way he might take to buying pictures or backing shows. And the ordinary businessman noted that the Big Businessman sat on orchestra and museum boards, and sparked university drives, and gave large sums to cultural projects; and noted too that his own architect son was doing as well financially as his other son in carpets.

Babbitt, as I have said, had been split up two for one: besides the fairly standard type, there was now an advanced type, a not at all Babbitty Babbitt. Of the standard sort there are still examples in plenty, most often among the not too big businessmen in not too big communities. Such fellows, once put in orbit, still revolve around a world of locker-room bourbon and poker-table smut, of the businessman's lunch table with its shop talk and political grumbling, of durable wisecracks and vestigial pieties, of handy-man putterings and hand-me-down hobbies, of Saturday night indelicacy and Sunday-morning decorum. Even these Babbitts acquire vivid glimpses of a world outside, through what their children take for granted or their wives would have a go at; though the wives can be the earlier breed too, using methods of looking young that suggest they never looked young, or of dressing well that suggest a vow to dress badly, and the sight of whom, dancing with their husbands or their friends' husbands in a Saturday-night world of rye-and-ginger-ale and harlequin glasses and wanton hips, somehow tells a great deal about their Tuesday mornings and their Thursday afternoons.

If Early Babbitt thus still flourishes, it is far less than he once did. A much more central figure is the un-Babbitty Babbitt, in part because so much has vanished, or receded, of the old Babbitt world. The businessmen's lunch club has been losing out to the executive's dining-room; the old atmosphere of private enterprise in a democracy has changed to something that, with its petty distinctions of rank and its telltale indications of favor, evokes Court life in a small 19th-century duchy. This Babbitt inhabits an Organization world with far fewer employers than Babbitt's had but with many more executives—a world that gives him numerous new and elegant claims to status but always, in the end, the status of an employee. Here, however philistine he may be in grain, he cannot solidify into the Babbitt of old unless he would petrify as well, and be discarded as dead wood. For if this new role is often just a revamping of the old one, it has so much extended its limits as not to tolerate Babbitt's old limitations. The conformity it insists on requires the lithest adaptability; the intolerances it imposes are not ignorant but informed ones; it demands the flying leap along with the docile lockstep, and a bland understanding smile as against stiff disapproving silence. For moving upward, here, means moving outward as well, into all regions of the corporation empire. The corporation empire is a real form of cosmopolitanism; and even at the fairly modest levels where Babbitt's true heirs may wind up, they may still have had jobs in four or five cities, taken trips to four or five countries, been not just city dwellers but suburbanites, summer residents, resort samplers; while as sound Organization Men they belong to much fewer organizations than Babbitt did. A dinkus in the lapel has given way to credit cards in the wallet, and via the credit cards has gone a life of plush hotels and restaurants and night clubs. And the new Babbitt must pursue a Good-Neighbor policy with Culture, never knowing when it may pay off: the spin of Babbitt's conversation can be as important as the cut of his clothes, and he must needs identify at sight a "list" that includes Stravinsky, Picasso, Bâtard Montrachet, *al dente*—but no, it's less a list than an oculist's chart. With each step further up in the world, he must be able to read a line further down on the chart: Courvoisier stands two lines above Le Corbusier, and Robert Frost one line above C. P. Snow. And the atmospheric shift from democracy to duchy involves the vital matter of a proper mate, of a wife who can be presented at Court and is indeed presentable generally—a wife who can put an insecure client's wife at ease, or herself at ease with a snooty one; who can display her chic but conceal her cleverness, be at home today with what till yesterday she'd never heard of, and be one of the girls, or one of the boys, while remaining a lady.

· 2 ·

This newer Babbitt, though but a step or two from meeting Culture on the landing, is yet not a quintessen-

((41))

tial figure of the New World. For elsewhere, by now, Business and Culture actually *have* met. Hostile to Culture a mere generation ago, Business today plays eager host to it; in fact, their relationship has not only its decided rapprochements, it has its amusing reversals. Like a married couple, the two are acquiring each other's characteristics. Culture, in a very real sense, is becoming Big Business: as against Industry's knack for making money, Culture has learned the art of raising it. This reversal is so complete that where the college receives from a big corporation five thousand shares of stock, the corporation's president receives from the college the degree of Doctor of Letters. I sometimes wonder how farfetched it is—or merely how far distant—to see a great symphony orchestra owned, flute, fiddle and snaredrum, by a great corporation; or the Metropolitan Opera, shall we say, owned by the Metropolitan Life; and so with graduate schools and art museums and libraries. And such arrangements might have fewer drawbacks than existing ones. Certainly the whole vexing, taxing matter of money-raising would be once for all abolished; problems of budgetry would be much curtailed; while matters of policy could largely be set straight at the outset. Perhaps this would be just another reversal, or reversion, to the world of the Court painter and the King's Mummers, but whatever its disadvantages, it would put an end to the savant turned salesman.

Actually the return to the world of patronage is already in effect—though on a modern rather than a

Medician basis—in the form of Foundations. A chief difference is that today patronage does not involve personal relationships; much, indeed, of the money that comes to Culture today comes from the dead. But even more of it comes from the living on perhaps the most attractive basis ever conceived for loving art, the most lucrative basis ever devised for practising philanthropy. There seems to me a first-rate Ph.D. thesis in American culture's precise indebtedness to the tax exemption; nay more, in its really vast dependence on it. Take this in conjunction with rich men's wills and it becomes almost literal truth that for the sustained support of Culture today, nothing's sure but death and taxes.

The alliance of Business and Culture is at its most beneficent in the endowments and Foundations that carry with them no shackling provisos on Business's part. Once this stops being true, trouble can enter; the voice is the voice of Culture but the hands are the hands of Business, or even the claws. The cost to Culture of what Business has achieved, say, on television, for Culture, raises a pretty point in double-entry cultural bookkeeping —and this, need I say, is a quite separate entry from what Business has achieved against Culture on television. But whatever the question of gain and loss by way of businessmen's fingers in the cultural pie, even larger is the question of gain and loss where those fingers are out of it. The question there, indeed, comes down to how much cultural pie there can even be. Consider the professional theatre, where Business does almost nothing for Culture and, since almost no one else does either, the theatre and Culture (in its pure state, at least) scarcely meet.

While Culture has been going into business, Business has been devising a culture of its own. Often the advertisements for a book are better written than the book itself: often advertising or publicity display real chic and gaiety, a wittily topical angle, a neat satiric touch. (This is not to be confused with those unbearably chichi and outré ads that no words can do injustice to.) Business hires well-known, and well-regarded, writers to turn out copy for it; or top show-music composers to do its TV jingles; or top illustrators and even famous painters to project its dreams—or at any rate those of its customers. Business, furthermore, trains people in all the arts of pleasing, in all the niceties of belonging, sends them ambassadorially forth to distant foreign capitals; and if the great corporations don't yet boast an actual poet- or painter-in-residence, they have certainly their social scientists in harness, their psychologists on call. And business leaders not only, thanks to lion-hunting wives, meet cultural bigwigs at dinner; they meet them by their own contrivance at lunch. Intelligence no longer looks askance at Intellect, Practicality no longer scoffs at Theorizing: beyond acknowledging their aura, Business often grasps their use.

As for Culture greeting Business, there is at times a sense of it not simply descending the staircase, but sliding palpitantly down the banister. It gets harder to understand what Culture's right true use should be, so quickly given—or driven—is it to wrong ones. This is not to be foolishly puristic about it: doubtless to drink one's Culture neat, one must retire to a hermit's cell. And Culture-and-soda can be a quite good drink, with a welcome element of bubbling sociability about it. But Culture-and-syrup is different; and Culture-and-arsenic is very different, not because if taken in daily doses it will prove fatal, but—quite the reverse—because in time it creates a Mithridatic immunity. In any case, Culture is being dispensed to more and more people in more and more hybrid forms, with more and more synthetic flavors, and with more and more doubtful effects; and by very personable and sinuous bartenders. No one a mere generation ago could have foretold how much miscellaneous knowledge millions of Americans would acquire just from listening to quizzes; nor have foreseen the endless airing of opinion on the air, the prodigious empire of open forums and before-breakfast classrooms and after-dinner controversies, the expounding of philosophy, the explaining of poetry, the analysis of music. It is virtually impossible today for any one who leafs through travel folders or is kept waiting by the dentist not to sop up some damp morsels of Culture. It is virtually impossible today for even uneducated people to be, in the old sense, ignorant—as it is virtually impossible for "educated" ones not to be in some sense misinformed.

But Culture is not knowledge, is only something dependent on it, something fortified by sound values, purified by sound taste. I use the word, thus far, as a kind of absolute, as expressing what makes for truly civilized living whether in society or in the self; I use the word as it emerges, say, in Culture and Anarchy. The culture of any particular time or place is of course something else, is the composite of all that works for and against Culture itself, of all that on the one side respects and on the other violates its essential disinterestedness. And the strange fact about American culture today is that Culture, by its alliance with Business, is in many ways working for the good of others, but at the cost of harm to itself. This is in part, but only in part, an inescapable corollary of the democratic process. It means, in a sense, that people know more than is good for them because they still do not know quite enough—that they have their taste no less corrupted than corrected by too much awareness of "taste"; that they become subservient to grammar while remaining ignorant of usage; abandon the engagingly coarse for the revoltingly refined; and, while despising the virtues of what they discard, debase the value of what they acquire.

But Culture and Demos is one thing, and Culture and Mammon is by and large another. The opportunities provided by democracy are among the supreme merits of our system of life; and by way of that system, Culture achieves some of her greatest victories among those at the outset uncultivated. With due allowance for all the academic required reading, or passion for uplift, or mere cultural shopping around, the response of this age to, say, classical records and quality paperbacks indicates a real thirst for more than mere thirst-quenchers. As for what is depressing about semi-educated taste, it can frequently of course be something transitional rather than terminal.

Culture's alliance with Demos is, in any case, a necessary risk boasting obvious rewards. Culture's alliance with Mammon may often seem indistinguishable from this—ours being, to the degree that the two words are of equal importance, a capitalist democracy, and ours thus being a society that couples education with material success. But the two alliances have vital points of difference. That with Mammon is for one thing more recent; is, for another thing, a conscious undertaking on Mammon's part; and, for another still, Mammon looks to the higher levels, Mammon's constitutes in fact an assault on a potential elite. Mammon, with his modern sense of enlightened self-interest, wants the best; as, with a modern sense of enlightened self-aggrandizement, he stands ready to pay for it. Mammon's motto, whether formulated or unconscious, appears to be "Take care of the talent, and the truckling will take care of itself." If this seems, on Mammon's part, monstrously cynical, it is also sufficiently realistic, born of experience with those whose kind of talent it would buy.

I use the word *talent* in a pretty literal sense, as meaning those with potentially striking gifts in words, ideas, imaginations, those able to make some mark or leave some dent on books or plays or movies or journalism, on design or décor, on humor or satire. In other words, I mean those who help create or modify the tone —social, esthetic, ultimately moral—of an age; *not* those who merely contrive its techniques. Our industrial need

((47))

for technicians, and the whole partnership of Business with Science, is something else, something much older, something born of America's practical Edisonian inventiveness, wherewith the Patent Office became a great anteroom to success.

In any case, Business had Science in harness long before it gave even a passing thought to Art; all this was so obvious as to be constantly satirized in the heyday of Main Street, and there is a good deal to be said for all this today, from how often we have used industrial advances for social progress. Mammon's alliance with the technicians necessarily preceded his alliance with the tastemakers, the knottier point being, did it really predestine it? (One recalls here Claude Bernard's "Art is I, Science is We.") In any case, the two alliances express between them a whole dominant side of our civilization —our merged gift of practical inventiveness and, as it were, of poetical salesmanship.

For we have got way beyond the old ideas of merchandising and advertising. Once upon a time the appeal was that the product was the best in its class, better than all its rivals; today the appeal may rest chiefly on how much better it is than its own last year's self. Once the appeal was solidly in intrinsic terms of comfort, enjoyment, durability, service—in other words, how much having it could help you; today it is subtly in terms of community leadership, social prestige, fashion pace-setting—of how much not having it can hurt you. Once its appeal was in terms of long wishing for it, of its being mouth-wateringly familiar; now it may well be something unheard of till yesterday, of its being enticingly exotic. And perhaps more than anything else, where once the appeal lay in making you contented with your lot, it now lies in keeping you tinglingly dissatisfied. The basis of every status symbol is that it must asperse the status quo, so that you not just live beyond your means; you heap scorn upon your memories. Wherever the standard of living enters in, the past—even the immediate past—is simply a slum.

All this has quite altered consumer psychology. Luxury merchandise and the urban market go in more and more for the snobbish overtone or cosmopolitan frame of reference. Styles of advertising and of packaging have sufficiently preyed on Culture to become, in themselves, a minor form of it. But Mammon's new alliance with Culture goes beyond the high-styled touch in salesmanship, it goes into the realm of Culture proper. There is a sense here of paying Paul to rob Peter, of giving more "art" to the packaging so as to give less of it to the product: certainly Mammon displays as promoter far more boldness and style than he does as sponsor or backer or editor.

Yet Mammon's writing hand is not in the end his whip hand. What is perhaps most significant about the new alliance is a sense of something atmospherically far more cultural but structurally far more Big-Businesslike. The new structure is eminently hierarchic, involving executive-above-executive-above-executive, so that everything the gifted copywriter or idea man does, or would like to do, must pass through a vast institutional postal service of IN and OUT boxes, a great meteorological region of prevailing cooler heads and counter-clockwise rumination and sudden storm clouds or squalls or frosts. It is, of course, the great magnitude of the operation that has created the whole new world, scarcely conceivable to *Main Street,* of Madison Avenue.

As the 1920s opened, commercial radio was in swaddling clothes and television unthought of; there were no opinion-polling organizations and few fact-finding ones; no huge talent agencies, no book clubs, no network music rights, no non-comic strips, no three-, four-, five-way package deals. Accordingly, today's opportunities for the bright, educated, arts-oriented young man are, compared with forty years ago, immensely greater; and are often more than opportunities, are outright invitations. For the right young men have been courted while still in college, receiving from desirable organizations in the outside world the kind of bids they once got from desirable ones on campus. Sometimes the right young men find the right young job, whether in teaching or research, or with a good magazine or publishing house or museum, but oftener the jobs they get are about equally composed of promise and menace, of opportunity and opportunism.

There are a lot of bright young men who want no part of this. However culturally plump, they are esthetically and morally fit and, like most such young men of forty years ago, they are anti-bourgeois. Quite often, of course, the need for a job can misdirect the choice of a career. But it is appalling how many good minds, and fruitful imaginations, are not just driven, but propel themselves toward the polluting stream; how many bright young talents are unblushingly pro-bourgeois. I don't mean in the sense that they are anti-bohemian—I mean that they are ultimately anti-cultural, ousting human values for creature success. They are the particularly melancholy offspring of Culture in the embraces of Mammon for, occurring at so posh a level, the seduction is of a truly perilous kind.

Babbitt was Babbitt, part of a world of business that stamped out no finer gifts in him. On the other hand, many of those who might have been part of a cultural aristocracy today populate Madison Avenue. And as between them and the Babbitts there is as distinct a difference in attitude as in level. For Babbitt in his confusions was not guileful but gullible, far less unbeliever than man of faith, and in fact a considerable romantic. But Madison Avenue's bright young men are not romantics in the least, are oftener realists of a depressing, a cynical kind; not even cynics of a Wildean cast, but such as *know* the value of everything but are yet guided in their decisions by the price.

Many of them—and of course Madison Avenue stretches nationwide—gave up too soon, stopped "growing" too early, for us to know how well they might have qualified for a world of high cultural values. But in their own way they often know all that their betters do, and sometimes more. They know more because, thanks to their jobs, they can afford more—more theatre and opera and ballet seats, more books and art books, more records and concert subscriptions, more trips abroad. Doubtless much of what they know comes in tenderized forms or cliché phrases, but much of it is solid and quite unpopularized and bespeaks appreciation no less than knowledge. The best of them talk your language, grasp you allusions, match your perceptiveness; and shipwrecked on an island with you, or even loafing aboard ship, can quite effortlessly assume your attitudes. They are a new race of Strasbourg geese richly stuffed with knowledge, whose livers Business presently will feed on. It is hard to believe what I was told as literal truth, that what certain courted young undergraduates most wanted to know was their potential employers' old-age benefits. And this seemed even more ironic than appalling, in view of how almost every day you read that this or that TV or publicity or agency executive is dead at 39 or 42 of a heart attack or a cerebral hemorrhage.

But dying early or living long, they highlight the reversed cultural direction of the past forty years, which must be termed in the end a real cultural defeat. For if many Babbitts now march under a less benighted banner and toward somewhat higher ground, from ground far higher there march energetically, emulously downward a host of bright young men.

Whatever Became of Personal Ethics?

Madison Avenue also, I imagine, is paved with good intentions. It would be strange if it weren't, what with exhibiting so many other likenesses to Hell, whether the temptations that bring men to it, or the torments after arriving. But Madison Avenue's paving stones represent *future* intentions as well as foiled ones: many of its residents mean some day to get out. Thus sang men once of Hollywood too, and of other pernicious settlements; and in truth men did get out, at least a few of them. This particular vow has perhaps been America's most costly illusion, a very graveyard of its culture. Unlike Europe, whose ruins are of stone and brick, ours are of chromium and grey flannel. Unlike Europeans, who can be stingy and sagacious about money, we are generous and suicidal. It is meant to save us hardship and it sentences us to Hell. Beyond that, our man-made hells are more insidious than Church-made ones: they are not merely punishments for temptations succumbed to, but are themselves full of temptations to boot. In the man-made hells, the Devil must forever contrive new treats and inducements, higher-paying work, grander-sounding titles. And man-made hells are much more understandable than Church-made ones, not just because they combine high pay with hard labor, but because it is easier to believe in your own weak nature than in a stern, retributive God. *How can I help it?* any child could understand, where *Why should He do this to me?* can seem quite unfathomable. Expiating guilt on God's terms is far more rigorous than learning to live with it on Freud's.

My point, however, is nothing so obvious as that psychoanalysis has become one of our great religions. My point is not about psychoanalysis at all, but only about a new shift by which people hold their guilt at bay. In today's business and professional world that employs the educated, the clever, the gifted—a world of air waves and advertising copy, of publicity and promotion, of newsprint and coated stock, of regional distribution and national circulation—great numbers of those recruited espouse a certain political and social philosophy. They are liberals. They have liberal objectives, vote liberal tickets, support liberal causes. They are genuinely social-minded; are unreservedly for integration, slum clearance, socialized medicine, prison reform; for old-age benefits and reclaimed young delinquents; for due process, for free speech, for the abolition of censorship. In a voting booth they are presumably their own man, in the club car only slightly the corporation's; they take off their blinkers after quitting their desks and their muzzles after leaving the building. A numerous group, they are necessarily of different selves and kinds. Some are violent about Southerners, some about Communists, some about Catholics. Some think practicality the most workable idealism; others fear that power corrupts, whatever its character. Some, worn out by the long grind, grow more militant in their liberalism; others, perked up by the new promotion, grow more perfunctory. But they are all liberals in no very ambiguous sense, on no quickly satirized terms.

Most of them indeed practice what they preach, at the town meeting as well as in the voting booth; in the books they buy, the warm-potato injustices they protest, and only a little less than formerly in the schools where they enroll their children. They firmly believe in the future. *Future,* as it happens, is the key word, the complicating word. For their own future marches side by side, as it were, with mankind's. Or rather, it fails to march side by side, from forever jockeying for position, jostling for precedence. These, after all, are the big futurity stakes, and *their* future can on occasion be at odds with mankind's. How bravely wave the banners of progress! How meanly read the inter-office memos! The contrast between the two is as sharp as that between the exalting dream and the shrilling alarm clock. And the conflict is as fierce as the contrast is pointed.

The schism they have made between the self and

society has somewhat the nature of a deal. The basis of the deal is not to hamper the self *in* society, not to make one's social ideals penalize one's personal welfare. Character, that is to say, must not stand in the way of career; belief must not always govern behavior. In a sense, of course, the new schism is as old as the human race; is the eternal clash between our acquisitive instincts and our aspiring ones, between the thrust of ambition and the prick of conscience. But in another sense there is perhaps something truly new about it; as there is further a real variation on something old.

What is perhaps new is what seems so contradictory. People who in the past led lives of educated careerism seldom espoused militantly social-minded aims. They often showed a proper community spirit or denounced political corruption in their own backyards; they favored hospitals and supported orchestras; they did much for growing children and something for wayward girls. But they seldom gave vocal support to social programs that reached beyond personal benevolence. They righted wrongs as against affirming rights; they did not plump for a social progress that might threaten their own. *Political* opportunists may have done so; or crusaders like the New England abolitionists who, as mill owners, were exploiters as well. But few business careerists have been open—and purse-open—liberals, rejecting all the arguments of a reasoned conservatism and hailing a future that should redress the wrongs of the past. What today's liberal careerists alone except from all this is the present. The present may require their groveling before the boss, or being a touch treacherous toward a colleague, or taking credit for some one else's bright idea, or transferring the blame for one's own mistake; it may require whooping up the network's clownish censorship or craven cancellations; it may demand a little polite job-lifting or sabotage or slander. But if it does, that springs from bondage to today's dog-eat-dog world and man-bites-man methods, and is in strong contrast to the forward-march into the future, to the crusade against all repression that doesn't obstruct promotion.

What seems new in this is not the fact of such a dichotomy, but its particular nature. Those who earlier aimed straight at success by however devious means always embraced a philosophy, or evolved an ethics, whereby they could glorify what they were doing. They found their sanction in an America that was the land of plenty, or in a democracy that was the gospel of opportunity, or in how hard knocks can strengthen character, or rough handling aid survival. And then, in the fullness of time, they crowned all this with septuagenarian largess. Many of them, indeed, managed to turn their ruthless careerism into "inspiring" careers: in any case, scarcely a one of them but hated Labor, fought humanitarian legislation, and branded social progress Communist.

Most past careerists did this from being a quite different breed from the one I would discuss. The new kind are a sort of debased intellectual class who, by way of their knowledge and skill, have become rather the writing hands of business than outright businessmen. Careers, for them, are not usually a tower to climb to the very top of, but a tunnel to work their way through, with plump economic security at the other end. These people have sought no philosophy to glorify their actions, have seldom rationalized their liberalism to mesh it with their livelihoods. They haven't even, a great many of them, turned hard; they are simply hardened to their roles; not least to New Dealing, as it were, from the bottom of the deck.

This means, as I have said, that in terms of liberal objectives, wherever possible they practise what they preach. And it is often possible—they can help their fellowman whenever he is segregated or jailed or flogged; censored or silenced; slum-dwelling or dispossessed. They only cannot when he is their colleague or competitor. And this seems new to me—a dog-eat-dog careerism that crusades for the underdog. What seems to me, along with it, a real variation on something old is that these people do steadily, quite early in life, what the hard-fisted rich used to do very late. For today's rat-racers, as they crowd other rats out of the race, suffer twinges of conscience; and so, when young and by way of their pay checks, they do what the Robber Barons once did when old and by way of their wills. They pay conscience money. But today's money, unlike yesterday's, is not paid retrospectively in leisurely remorse; with their knack for being modern, they have evolved Pay-as-you-go Penance.

· 2 ·

Here, as so often today, we must pull up to greet the
national villain in all this, the notorious Bitch-Goddess.
Moreover, it's very easy to excoriate success once we
dub it a rat race; easy to condemn it when we spell out
its origins and techniques. But in fairness we ought not
to forget how long and how rousingly, from pulpits and
rostrums, in language eminently exalted and only moderately vague, Success was made part of bright democratic
vistas, of the fulfillment of self and the furthering of
progress. We must not forget for how long, before it became the Bitch-Goddess, it was the great affirmative
gospel of American life. Realistically judged, our carrying that gospel too far—along with not grasping that as a
"democratic" ideal it was no match for a capitalist im-
perative—could not but bring about what prevails today. Also, as higher education became one of democracy's great dividends, it could not but be reinvested in
material enterprise—at length in Organization enterprise, with the rivalries now painfully intramural, the
coveted job not a mile away but across the hall, the war
a civil war, the rat racers brother rats.

Along with all this, something resulted that I don't
want to exaggerate but that, taking even a most moder-
ate view, seems very disquieting. There resulted, among
far too many intelligent and educated people, the sub-
stitution of social morality for personal ethics. This seems
to me a menacing contemporary phenomenon, with even
a sort of Communist fillip about it—the fillip of the end

justifying the means, of men being entitled to finagle so long as other men shall be promised their chance. It has also led to having many *really* enlightened people so much stress social morality as seldom to refer to personal ethics. This to some extent may be the result of their taking personal ethics for granted; or of their assuming that as social morality advances, personal ethics must also. But I suspect that it measurably results from something else—from a feeling that personal ethics, as a specific exhortation, reeks of both copybook maxims and conservative class thinking. But surely, when liberalism can seem more a sop to conscience than a sign of it, it is time to shift emphasis a little.

Perhaps the best quality of old-fashioned conservatism was its sense of personal honor. The phrase "personal honor" so smacks of code that a dozen years ago one shied away from it, a generation ago even tended to mock it. One would still prefer a phrase like "personal decency"; but the two are not the same, and it is perhaps the very idea of code that now weighs in honor's favor. For the decent man largely *lacks* the prejudices that becloud social vision—where the honorable man behaves well in spite of having them. What was too often amiss with personal honor was its restricting itself to a group or class or nation; was its becoming, at its worst, the Southern-gentleman or old-school-tie kind of thing. But, purged of class limitations, it remains a final touchstone of conduct—first, from its governing regardless of personal bias, from its operating toward enemy no less than friend; and again, from its being born of inner pride and self-respect. To take unfair advantage or use ungenerous means shamed oneself; and on this score—of its creating no guilt or self-contempt—it made for a healthier society, or at least a healthier basis for one. Personal honor, to be sure, often rested on wealth dishonorably gained, and could constitute a kind of luxury ideal. But it operated, and still operates, among all classes, in all sorts of communities: where it all too little operates today is in the intelligent, educated world I am speaking of.

Well, we need not bring back the phrase, with its unwelcome overtones of caste; "personal ethics" will do very nicely. But, observing the steep decline of the thing itself in a "liberal" society, we must have *some* phrase to express it. Think just of surface manifestations today—think of the pokes and sideswipes among all sorts of news personalities; think of the snideness and malice, in public, of all sorts of "superior" people, self-righteous as well as self-seeking. Liberals, almost all of them. Many of them may be nothing more than decidedly touchy and pushy; others nothing worse than compulsively opportunist; doubtless only one in five is really adept at character assassination or at knife-in-the-back. Broadway, for example, abounds in social-minded, cause-conscious people; Broadway resists reaction, opposes censorship; but Broadway provides a proverbially well-lighted stage for the envenomed ego and the venal claw.

Here again we must pull up—to admit that anxiety stalks the scene hardly less than ambition. A frequent defensive plea, among such opportunists themselves, is that the jettisoning of ethics isn't merely callous or cynical, but cruelly deterministic; that in so fierce a struggle the lust to succeed is more than half the need to survive. There is no way to cry "Hold, enough!" Even should you not breathe down the neck of the man ahead of you, the man behind is breathing down yours. Certainly there is truth in all this; not least in the final twist that has made of careerism something where, if you *don't* win a prize, you must pay a forfeit. But it is not the whole truth, nor need it be elevated into a law.

All this, it must surely be clear, has no more to do with attacking liberalism than decrying Sunday Christianity has to do with attacking faith. The morality involved, it seems to me, can be worse than conscience-money morality; can be pure escapist morality, and escapist in two ways. For, however real these people's sympathy with the diverse victims of society, the fact remains that the victims nowhere impinge on these people's world, nowhere threaten it. And there is the second fact that toward all such victims these people can feel a beneficent guilt, a wholly impersonal guilt—for the wrongs done here are done by others, where the wrongs done closer to home all too often are not. Protesting one kind of misbehavior while indulging in a different kind is familiar enough; here, coming from people who do much to shape present-day conduct, it can be all too dangerous as well.

For if, *on their present terms*, these people help create a future victory for social values, it must smack of defeat as well. If people so relatively high-placed more and more shrug off personal ethics, must not other people soon regard doing so as normal? And on that basis what kind of "superior" individuals will inhabit the social-minded world of the future? For that matter, how social-minded can it be—how far can social reform prove a match for personal ruthlessness? Won't we, rather than abolishing the rat race, have simply made it available to everybody? Already there exist TV spokesmen for liberalism whose programs get gossipy and personal and who, while enjoying large incomes from the programs, pay their panelists nothing. Already there are Broadway big shots who have sound enough social ideas, but who can behave like monsters. Already we have newspapers that, under the guise of being humane about what disturbs and distorts people, exploit every humiliating, distorting detail. Even at higher levels, what chance have social goals against careerist finish lines? What price equality when intelligent human beings claw one another for a foot-and-three-eights of precedence, or for billing half an inch larger? By all means let us extend, wherever possible, every form of social endeavor. But how ultimately great is the gain to bring up children with no prejudice against race and with every sympathy for the poor, if they are to have no scruples against back-stabbing, and an utter apathy toward fair play?

·II·

◆◆◆◆◆◆◆◆◆◆◆

Our Unhappy Happy Endings

ANY ENTERPRISING young American with his fortune to make might consider setting up in a small way as a manufacturer of rose-colored glasses. The market for them is great already, and said to be increasing; there is even, I gather, a particular market for rose-colored glasses that can also increase astigmatism or induce myopia. And people have been told that soon they can have a pair that not only softens the landscape but also blots part of it out.

For the world (as who does not know) has grim sights to offer today and may be offering grimmer ones tomorrow. Any moment, for example, there may be earth satellites galore, though no longer any earth. And together with frightening things to see, there are all the new facilities for seeing them more clearly: what with the light shed by sociology in one place, and science in another, and medicine in a third, truth—or at any rate the exposure of error and the collapse of illusion—everywhere confronts us. And not every one likes this; the liking for Truth, let alone the dedicated search for it, is not extensive. Truth is a luxury item, not a mass-consumed commodity; and if the truth about the world is never in great demand, how much less—despite the influence of the Freuds—is the truth about oneself. Actually, people will clutch at the truth about what a cruel, cold, dog-eat-dog world this is as an excuse for turning their backs on the truth about themselves; but this, if it lessens their feeling of guilt, still leaves them uneasy: they would rather turn their backs on both things.

I am speaking for the most part of the situation in America, which differs from that of Europe. Unlike Europe, America has for a long time lived in a prospering present, with the sense of an even more prosperous future. There have been depressions; but materially, the American dream has been nourished by America's waking hours. Given such a Land of Plenty, is it not perforce a Land of Promise as well? In a country where any one can become president, every one will dream of becoming president—if not of the U.S., then at least of U.S. Steel. In a country, again, where making money is so much a national talent that 2 x 2 can overnight just as easily be 4000 as 4, a sense of realism is not likely to prevail. In America the facts of life, as borne out by reams of statistics, by thousands of careers, are every bit as resplendent as the fantasies. In spite of periodic depressions and of world events, the happy ending has become a reigning American myth because it is demonstrably no myth at all. Things may differ in a Europe of collapsing economies, violent usurpations, bombed-out and blood-stained recollections, weary bones and protesting bellies. There the sense of reality is far more insistent; there, one always built castles in Spain from living in France. Or, struggling in Poland or Ireland, one looked to America as a real-life solution; there, escapism involved an actual escape. With us, it is rarely even a genuine transcendence; it is the merest transference; it more and more means TV glimpses not of castles in Spain but of penthouses on Park Avenue, not of fairyland but of twenty-times-our-own-income land: if we are perhaps the most unrealistic of nations today, we are at the same time perhaps the least romantic.

In a land like ours, of such unquestionable—and un-questioned—plenty, with most people not many escapist visions of their own are needed; nor, in a land of incessant sales talks, are very many allowed. Wildy escapist as we are in our thought processes, we are just as timidly so in what we project. It is all peculiarly recognizable, local, life-sized escapism, a matter of Cadillacs and mink coats, of flood-lighted swimming pools and soft-lighted boudoirs, of executive suites and headwaiter salaams; it is a world, in fact, where pushbuttons do virtually everything that magic carpets once did. Even our daydreams have a way of carrying price tags and including commercials. With ours the most advertised as well as affluent of existences, we tend less and less toward moonlit mysterious romanticizings and more and more toward high-priced vicarious living. I know all the fine things TV has done and is capable of doing, what an education it can be for the young, and what a blessing for the old, and what a godsend for the house-bound; all the same, it seems to me the greatest cultural calamity in this country's history. And not, as might be supposed, because it has so cut down on reading and reflection, or become a vicious drug-like habit—true and bad though both things are; but rather because it has so enormously increased our escapist instincts while so crucially cheapening our escapist symbols. Instead of magic casements opening on a faery world—which even the movies in some degree provided —television offers authentic close-ups of affluent real life, authentic lowdowns on luxurious highlife. Its happy endings are not of the old fairy-prince sort, or so very often of Boy-Meets-Girl; they are of a you-too-can-play variety all too often concerned not with romance or heroism or *gloire*, but with give-away merchandise and quiz-show hauls and commercialized competitions, with people leaping to dangerous ephemeral fame or to ruinously surtaxed fortune, the sort of thing you look at on Tuesday and by Friday week may very well be competing for yourself.

The old daydreams, I would think, were healthier in kind and less harmful in effect: even the victims of the old gilded twaddle seldom mistook it for truth. Such stuff, indeed, wore the magic cloak of impossibility. Today's daydreams do not; they don't need a miracle to come true, all they need is a break. At the same time, in a world of

candid-camera intimacy and of owner-authorized close-
ups and of spotlighted keyholes, all sense of distance has
been annihilated, hence the enchantment lent by distance has vanished. For one reluctant Garbo there are a
thousand palpitant publicity seekers. The highly possible
daydreams, the do-it-yourself happy endings, have a
plausible real-life air; but just because they make us so
competitive, they themselves become more compulsive.
They are not just part of our dreaming, they are part of
our thinking. And all this, for another reason too, may
very well be in our blood. Since the United States itself
constitutes the greatest success story in the history of nations, the success story is part of our heritage, has everywhere colored our psychology. And we have come to
equate it with happiness, partly because we pretty much
believe there can be no happy ending without material
success, partly because we tell ourselves that *with* material success, we can reorder and elevate our lives. The
very reassuring idea in all this is that once you have
money, you can quite truthfully affirm that money isn't
everything.

If, as I have said, mass-mind daydreams are not too
difficult of fulfillment in a thriving democracy, then the
very dreaming will be along fulfillable lines. Hence our
nationally nursed happy ending has followed the success
story rather than the self-development or the heroic-
achievement or the love-in-a-cottage story (indeed this
last, in an atmosphere with the slightest sophistication, is
apt to invoke a snicker). To be sure, we do respond to an
ending that combines a higher self with a bigger income;

but "All for love and the world well lost"—or all for country, or for God—seems a little excessive as well as unreal. We exult in something not only more down-to-earth but also more just-around-the-corner, more local-boy-makes-good. Our Van Cliburns delight us not just because they are so talented, or even so Texan, but because of how sensationally their talent pays off.

Now, if the good thing about an immensely affluent democracy is how often it lets dreams come true, the not so good thing is that far more people will go in for such dreams than can ever fulfill them; and the not much better thing is that, with so many people competing, even for the winners there must be frightful tensions and ruthless techniques. There is no secret to any of this: it is all too well known that the happy ending in America can involve very unhappy preliminaries, that the photo finish we dote on is often the photo finish of a rat race. Nor are the unhappy preliminaries the kind of trumped-up snags and romantical setbacks they once were: mass-medium fiction today often sticks quite close to real life, to un-Tarkingtonian adolescence, to un-Derring-Do sensationalism, to the realistic headache that follow marriage, not the romantic heartaches that precede it. The story, *except for the happy ending,* is often all too plausible, identifiable, disturbing—a genuine problem play or novel. It knows the real score, regardless of its last-minute fictional home-run. Indeed, it knows the real score so well that the home run is less an old-fashioned sop than a present-day necessity. For we are neurotically haunted today by the imminence, and by the ignominy, of failure.

We know at how frightening a cost one *succeeds:* to fail is something too awful to think about.

This is the most unwholesome, the most degrading aspect of our life today: that the harshly competitive terms, the overwhelmingly materialistic standards of success—as most Americans would define success—rob failure of all distinction and even all dignity. The happy ending is so much needed because the unhappy ending is so genuinely painful—a matter of being squeezed out, sucked dry, looked down on, pushed under, thrown on the scrap heap, smuggled into a sanitarium. And so succeed we must, at all cost—even if it means being a *dead* millionaire at fifty.

The need for such happy endings is, I would suggest, a symptom of an anxiety-ridden culture ("One way of getting an idea of our fellow-countrymen's miseries," said George Eliot, "is to go look at their pleasures"); certainly a symptom of something more acquiescent than affirmative. At any rate, it would seem no accident that during ages of great human adventurousness, of great humanistic advancement, of great creative drive—a Periclean Athens or an Elizabethan England—tragedy has always flourished and been prized, life has been looked at unflinchingly for what it is, yet has at the same time seemed more than life-sized. The heroic downfall had something exultant, not shoddy or self-pitying about it; and just as the protagonists of great tragic drama spurned comfortable solutions, so their audiences needed no last-minute consolations. "Those nations are happy," Lord Acton remarked, "which do not resent the complexity of life."

There are, of course, good happy endings as well as bad ones, but surely they are of a kind that in some way expresses happiness rather than glibly promises it. What seems to me so disquieting is that our current happy endings rarely have to do with happiness itself. They emphasize not the victory but the spoils. They reveal people not profiting by their own mistakes but capitalizing on other people's. They show people not rising above their surroundings but coming to terms with them. It would seem that there is very little nobility left, even in America's daydreams.

Fashions in Vulgarity

NOTHING, in a sense, would be easier to chronicle than a history of bad taste. The past is strewn with horrible examples; we need only look at the drearier or declining sections of cities, or in junk or antique shops, or—since on occasion vulgarity begins at home—in our own family attics. There are McKinley-period trophies in architecture, German-beermug-era trophies in décor. Everywhere there are reminders of a false refinement; or novels that ladies quite as much as ladies' maids once wept over. Every age yields fictional accounts of moneyed upstarts—Trimalchio in ancient Rome, M. Jourdain in seventeenth-century France, the Veneerings in nineteenth-century England. Was "bad taste" ever more rife than among Victorian England's indigestible wedding-cakes in stone? Yet, was "vulgarity" ever so ridiculous as with the great Lord Chesterfield, who deemed it vulgar to laugh aloud; or with the French classical drama, that forbade mention of the handkerchief, since on its exalted stage not noses were blown, but trumpets.

Yet, though nothing were more easily compiled than a chronicle of bad taste, nothing, after a time, calls out more for revision. Let fifty years go by, and it is not the items in the catalogue that shriek bad taste; it is the cataloguer. Not what he excoriated will seem vulgar, but what he extolled. In the early 1920's a critic of décor, championing the most functional furniture, might have whacked away at the curlycued accessories of the Victorians. Today all too many people wish their keepsakes had been kept, sigh in vain for their grandparents' square pianos and rosewood sofas; and shudder at the metal frames and tubular stems that passed for furniture. Clearly, since taste began, one generation's fashion has become the next generation's fright.

In the degree, then, that it posits touchstones and untouchables, proclaims What's Done and proscribes What Will Never Do, every catalogue of bad taste is a comedy of over-assurance. Virtually the same era that banished the handkerchief from the drama, and laughter from the drawing-room, cheerfully made butts of cuckolds and sport of madmen. The Augustans, while thinking it effeminate for men to carry umbrellas, deemed it manly for them to carry muffs. The Victorians, while forbidding mention of most illnesses and all sex, doted on rancid practical jokes. Yet, for all such warnings of booby traps, there is perhaps some point in our trying to discover vulgarity's more permanent traits. From the past, we get at least a clue in its verbal alliances, in the company it kept.

There was once constant reference to "vulgar display," to "vulgar curiosity," to "vulgar presumption." Vulgar display, probably the arch offender, calls up visions of too much finery and jewelry, of bric-a-brac and be-silvered-and-china'd dining-room tables—or simply of too much dinner. All this particularly brings the last century to mind, for with it emerged large, prosperous middle-class families that, by requiring large houses, encouraged lavish living. Moreover, an age that admired plump, high-busted women put no tax on heavy meals. Then, too, so prudish an age banned so many other forms of indulgence as perhaps to make lavishness less an initial desire than a kind of last resort. A respectable matron dared not smoke a cigarette; on the other hand she could virtuously eat three slices of cake.

Actually, even the more tasteful Victorians never stigmatized display in itself; they merely stigmatized this thing or that on display. Passing up, for the moment, any distinction between vulgarity and bad taste, we still might note that vulgarity isn't avoided merely through good taste in individual selection; there must also be a sense of proportion about the whole. Nor need we confine ourselves to the marble and plush atrocities of upstarts: the desire to exhibit on a vast scale has much ancient and aristocratic warrant. Most lordly establishments impart a too strutting sense of ownership, of greedy heaping-up and senseless size. Measured against a perfect taste, the patrician's giving material form to his pride of rank can be just as vulgar as the parvenu's proclaiming his lack of any.

There was that other once-common phrase, "vulgar presumption." It has largely fallen into disuse, not because people have stopped being presumptuous but because the phrase became a caste reproof—something applied to whomever one deemed one's social inferior. The culprit might often be vulgar enough, whether from a bumptious attempt to get on or a blatant attempt to dazzle; but he was hardly presumptuous: it was rather his detractors who presumed. But of course the class bias that stamps so many things vulgar goes very deep—indeed to the roots of the word itself, to *vulgus* or the common people. Something, in other words, was vulgar that had a lower-class stamp—or at least the stamp of a lower class than one's own.

This class bias is not uninstructive; but though we have still to define vulgarity, plainly in its subtler connotations today it has not just overflowed "lower class" banks; it has been rechanneled in a different direction. We might even contend that it is only the common people —along with some decidedly uncommon ones—who are not vulgar. What were once designated the lower orders may be coarse or crude, may indeed be common or cheap or disgusting. But the things they do that are most beyond the pale—belch or spit, eat with their knives or sleep in their underwear—do not quite fit our current sense of "vulgar." It is crude to eat with your knife; what is vulgar is to drink tea with your little finger extended. It is disgusting to pick your teeth; what is vulgar is to use a gold toothpick. It is illiterate to say "aint I"; what is vulgar is to say "aren't I." The common people, as a group, are not vulgar if only because they don't know enough or care enough to be.

It is among those who would once have been termed their betters that we encounter vulgarity full blast. We encounter it, that is, when signs of education have entered in; when there is a certain awareness of social or cultural or esthetic right and wrong; when there is a craving to attract notice or seem to belong. We are never, said La Rochefoucauld, so ridiculous through the qualities we have as through those we pretend to; and we are never, he might have added, so cheap. For, together with such pretensions, there almost always goes the attempt to mask them—the coy tactic, the devious maneuvre. Vulgarity, I would think, involves motivation. People are vulgar when, for self-interested reasons, they resort to unworthy methods—whenever they do something to falsify or floodlight their prestige or importance, their claims to position or talent or knowledge. They are equally vulgar when, from the same kind of motives, they fail to do something. One of the columnists told of a Broadway figure who displayed a new gold cigarette case. "I'm sick of gold," he remarked—"what I'd have really liked was a platinum cigarette case: but my friends would have thought it was silver."

At an innocuous level, vulgarity is mere vanity—people's wanting to look their best, or better than their best. Oliver Cromwell might exhort the portraitist to paint him warts and all; most of us desire to have the warts removed, and dimples added. Few of us speak as readily of the ancestor who was hanged as of the ancestor who was knighted. But if we weren't a little vulgar in matters of this sort we might be something much worse, we might be unbearably priggish. It is not till people, in manifesting superiority, begin to seem sniffy and cheap —or no better than what they disparage—that vulgarity turns offensive. The well-placed have for generations made a vulgar ploy of vulgarity: Jones, they will remark, had "the bad taste" to refer to something they didn't want mentioned; or Smith had "the insolence" to remind them of something they preferred to forget. This sort of high-handedness always has vulgar blood; high-handedness, indeed, must pass an esthetic test of being more stylish or witty than it is arrogant and rude. Equally, there are right and wrong snubs. The wrong ones can be as illbred as anything they wish to pulverize. For a nice snub, con-sider the very nobly born Frenchman to whom some one not half so wellborn was bragging of his vast family man-sion with its great high-domed dining-room. "With us," the Frenchman finally murmured, "it's just the other way. Our dining-room is so low that all we can eat is fried sole."

Obviously, there are ways in which human and artis-tic vulgarity differ. Vulgarity in life is not just an esthetic offense; it has a falseness or impurity about it, an *inner* cheapness. Vulgar people often display perfect form; can talk well, live smartly, even get discreetly ahead in the world. But as they grow superficially more presentable, they grow, if anything, inwardly more insensitive. There is even a kind of vulgarity so self-assured as to take pride in flaunting itself: a very famous theatre personage sent out, as a Christmas card, a picture of himself posing for a beer ad. Vulgarity in art, on the other hand, usually involves form as well as substance, and questions of esthetic effect. But it, too, largely derives from a false or flashy motive, from a greater wish to be impressive than sound. Often in men of much talent we find a streak of it —of excess or exhibitionism, specious beauty or spurious virtue. Swinburne can be too lilting or lush; Wilde and Disraeli use too much pomade; Tennessee Williams can be lavishly sensational, William Saroyan ostentatiously humane.

On the other hand, we must distinguish between styles in art and the vulgarization of a style. Thus, gingerbread architecture with its childlike Hansel-and-Gretel playfulness may be far less vulgar than "classical" mansions that look like U.S. subtreasuries. One may not respond to the baroque of Tiepolo's frescoes or Prandtauer's architecture; but except where misapplied, baroque is not vulgar in the least. Indeed, the real test of taste perhaps only arises at the level of the ornamented or theatrical. Any one, by playing safe, by wearing only grey and navy blue, by sticking to the best Georgian spoons, by reading Virgil or Racine, can be unassailably tasteful. The test of taste comes in one's particular use of bright paint and loud colors, or harps and trumpets, or marble and jewels. Almost any one can grasp the vulgarity in Liszt and the lack of it in Mozart; it is more difficult to grasp the vulgar lapses in Wagner and the lack of them in Berlioz. And certainly one great form of vulgarity is the fear of vulgarity; it flaws the work of even a Henry James.

· 2 ·

Vulgarity does not stand still: there are fashions in it, it shows progress, it gains on one front and loses on another. The world of today differs strikingly from that of two centuries ago—machinery and mass production, literacy and mass communication, democracy and relatively classless living have proved banes and blessings alike. Material display—the overmuch, the over-large, the over-stuffed, the over-shiny—has in great part been streamlined into submission. Our material tastes have not only learned from the excesses of the past, they are shaped by the exigencies of the present. What with a general lack of space today, and lack of servants; with doctors and diets, with the rise of sport and decline of prudery, most people eat, dress, live, travel, entertain more simply. To gorge or splurge is curiously unchic. Most people indeed live like most other people, in a world of deep-freezes, dishwashers, station wagons, casseroles and baby-sitters. A pantry maid is almost as remote as a coach-and-four; and a man may see the same dress on his secretary as on his wife. And with so much social and cultural leveling off, vulgar display has steeply declined.

The new vulgarity is different. The old vulgarity followed that classic rule for the playwright—always show rather than tell. The vulgar used to show how grand they were by the size of their houses, the massiness of their plate, the snootiness of their butlers; by how they overdressed, over-tipped, overrode those about them. They never said they were rich; they never had to.

Today the old stage formula has been discarded for the blunter vulgarity of *announcing* one's importance. Self-display has passed over into self-advertisement; and it is not so much the business world that conducts itself so as the world of journalism, of Hollywood and Broadway, of TV and "the communication arts." In that world people, beyond frequently engaging paid publicists, distribute their own testimonials, write their own plugs, sing their own praises, stress their own good deeds. And when not patting their own backs, they are slapping—or stabbing—other people's. When they cannot command the limelight, they invade it. This is an age of name-dropping —and of last-name-dropping even more—when on meeting a famous man of sixty, a man of twenty-four straightway calls him Bill. And as the first name flourishes in speech, so does the first person in writing. Serious writers turn out waggish pieces as a way of plugging their books. Columnists brag, when the most piffling news story breaks, how they had predicted it months before. Into the body of their newspaper stints people inject commercials about their TV appearances. Even all sense of occasion has vanished. At a small private New Year's Eve party, while the guests were watching, on TV, the crowds gathered in Times Square, one television man sang out loudly to another: "They wanted *me* to handle this—but we couldn't get together on the dough." The remark, to be sure, isn't much more vulgar than the sort of gathering that makes it possible. In the professional world today, entertainment tends to be the merest form of self-advancement, of blandly feeding the mouth that bites

((83))

you, of managing to be seen, of striking up useful connections on sofas, of cooking up deals over drinks. Even those hostesses who are above the battle and imagine they are exhibiting lions are actually racing rats.

All this, however appalling, is today perhaps inevitable. What with ratings and samplings, press-agentry and polls, people who are supposed to mold and influence others must more and more promote themselves, make shop-windows of their offices, show windows of their homes. Truman Capote, in his book about the visit of the *Porgy and Bess* troupe to the Soviet Union, told how, while most of those on board the train going into Russia relaxed and joked, a columnist was kidded for sitting in a compartment alone, pounding relentlessly away at his typewriter. "People don't get into my income-tax bracket," he explained, "by looking at scenery."

Furthermore, the whole fashion in entertaining, or interviewing, or "educating" mass audiences today tends to throw privacy to the winds, to make publicity not just an unreprehensible, but a greatly respected, side of modern life. To use zoological terms once more—it keeps getting harder to use strictly human ones—there now goes on a kind of human horse show, in which blue-ribboned personalities are trotted up and down, are photographed, queried, televised; or are just put on view as distinguished hosts or pedigreed hostesses endorsing Scotch or bed-sheets or soap. For the amateurs in all this, the appeal to vanity may be enough: for the professionals, it is part of a fierce struggle to survive. Big-name feuding is no longer mere internecine strife; it is a spectator sport.

Which of two feuders will come out ahead is on a par with which of two football teams.

The worst part of all this is that it has *become* such a spectator sport. It was said, long ago, that evil communications corrupt good manners: it might be said more pertinently today that mass communication corrupts good manners, that we are all being gradually worn down, that without even being aware of it, we are acquiescing in what would have appalled us twenty-five years ago. And how not, with the very air we breathe commercialized, with the very lives we live treated as so much copy? Quite literally, it is the gossip columnist's business to write about what is none of his business. The quiz programs with their venal lure and test-of-virtue stakes have vanished; but another kind of quiz program survives, where interviewers ask people—before millions of listeners—questions that their closest friends might hesitate to ask them when alone.

It is perfectly true that it takes two to make up such interviews—and millions, listening in, to make a go of them. Clearly, were there no people willing to be questioned, and no large audiences intent upon the answers, such programs could not exist. But, psychologically and sociologically, the thing is not so simple. With the person interviewed, vanity; love of the limelight; the fear that it will go elsewhere, are strong inducements; and in an age when publicity has become respectable and when psychiatry has licensed people to Tell All, fewer and fewer are those who when invited will say No. But what has happened to the performer is really less important than what has happened to the public. Of course, the average person is full of curiosity and enjoys gossip. But to argue that —because he's something of a peeping tom—it's his inquisitiveness that produces such interviews, is pure peeping-tommyrot. We bring up our children, we order our lives, we regulate our society on the contrary principle that our shoddier instincts should not be deliberately pandered to. Those most genuinely concerned for freedom of speech are no less concerned for the right of privacy; nor are they misled when sensationalism appears purporting to be the servant of truth, or when psychiatry is commercially invoked to chaperone smut. The motive of the scandal magazines is all too clear. It is where the motive is masked, when privacy is invaded on the pretext of a sociological search warrant, that a more menacing vulgarization appears; and as the product of such corrupting alliances, what sort of children will inhabit the world of tomorrow? For in time values not only get tarnished: they even get turned around. A few years ago George S. Kaufman, by complaining that *Stille Nacht* was being turned into a kind of cheap Christmas commercial, roused a storm of furious protest against himself: in the face of such things, who shall dare to argue that people can distinguish God from Mammon?

We live in a world where TV is now sovereign, is so enthroned that 50,000,000 Americans sit bareheaded before it for hours on end, enduring blare for the sake of glare, and forever plagued by those powers behind the throne—the sponsors with their intrusions. *Of course* there are good television programs; but that is sociologically beyond the point. The point is that for tens of millions of people TV has become habit-forming, brain-softening, taste-degrading; has altered for the worse the whole cultural climate of American life. Privacy was in sufficient danger before TV appeared; and TV has given it its death blow. And as all liking for privacy vanishes, all dislike of publicity must vanish too. Men that one would have supposed had distinction are nowadays Men of Distinction by way of the ads. Indeed, the better known a man is for his taste or good character, the more he is sought out, the more he is importuned, to sully or betray them. When those who shape our manners shout at parties about not getting together over the dough, or send out their beer blurbs as Christmas cards, who shall maintain that the vulgarity that once featured a clock planted in a Venus de Milo's belly has disappeared? Some of us might even put back the clock if we could.

Some Notes on New York

TREATED AS ANYTHING at all personal, as anything not just a sociological study, New York—by which I here mean Manhattan—is apt to emerge a blind-men-and-the-elephant kind of enterprise. Furthermore, one's sense of period must affect one's approach scarcely less than one's sense of place; and perhaps what one is looking for as much as what one professes to find. And New York is a great plus-and-minus city that can get into your blood but also under your skin and that, in Apple-of-Discord fashion, can have the gift of making one dissatisfied with other cities rather than enamored of itself.

New York is at once cosmopolitan and compartmented, without a unifying culture. Unlike London or Paris, it has no relatively homogeneous population; has —for all classes—almost no shared history or shaping traditions; for that matter, it has almost no landmarks, no backwaters, no reminders. Today's middle-aged New Yorker who would "preserve" his New York past must live a virtual fantasy life. Gone, quite as much as the El or the open-top bus, are the Village, the upper West Side, whole parts of midtown as he knew them; almost all the old-time restaurants and small shops with a history; six-day bicycle races as well as Giant-Dodger feuds; the Lafayette as well as the old Brevoort, the old Ritz as the Murray Hill, the Century Theatre as the Empire; and the Met is going. As one difference that could do for ten, Piccadilly Circus remains substantially what it was; Times Square is now a shop-windowed slum.

There has come about another great change. To the trite fact that most New Yorkers weren't born in New York must be added the fact that most New Yorkers no longer live there, either; that they themselves look upon it as "a nice place to visit." They live in other boroughs, in towns close by, in suburbs or Exurbia; and except as they work in Manhattan, they use it, like the rest of the country, for its restaurants, theatres, night clubs, museums, luxury shops. As for the modest-income New Yorker who lives with a wife and three children in Flushing, he perhaps doesn't see the city after working hours twice a year. To be sure, almost all big cities have been decentralized. Yet in most of them one may live way out in the suburbs and will still identify with the city itself, will still have a sense of roots and actual ties, will belong to civic as well as suburban organizations, will vote for city officials, be concerned with city politics. But you can live fifty minutes from the Manhattan you work in and have no other connection with it.

The change, with New York, is not simply sociological

—population explosion; decentralization; fiercely contested island space. The change is increasingly cultural—a very *atmosphere* of change. The city's cosmopolitanism argues movement, transience, novelty; means, in addition to a city, a kind of permanent World's Fair. Thanks to Jets, people from all over the world, people who influence taste and thought, who promote things, who perform, pour constantly in and out of New York to make it the most dynamic passing show, and even one-night stand, in history. There is such a rapid, incessant interchange of ideas, impressions, witticisms, faces, fads, such a clearing-house of news, that at a party in Manhattan the guests can easily swap accounts of parties the night before in London, Brussels, San Francisco and Rome, offering political scuttlebut no less than social gossip. New Yorkers and Londoners in government, society, the professions, the arts, have so much become part of one world that it hardly matters which is the home team and which the visiting one. And inside a generation much that is Londonish has been sprayed over New York, and even more that is New Yorkish has been infused into London. If London is changing faster now, there is much more for it to change from. *Londoners*, in any case, don't change as fast as New Yorkers: if only for class or sentimental reasons, many London *habits* refuse to change at all.

London, moreover, remains a man's city where New York is chiefly a woman's. London has whole streets that cater to men's wants. It has its great solid phalanx of fortress clubs. It has Parliament, and Downing Street, and all that goes with them. Although Englishmen love the country and hurry off to it, they can have a distinctive town life too. Comparable New Yorkers have to go to the country for their real enjoyments—only to lead there, not country weekends but country-club ones. The country, even then, can be a kind of branch office, with one's bridge partner one's business partner, one's golf partner one's best client. But what, at a more intelligent and cultivated level, crucially distinguishes New York from London or Paris or Rome is that it is a commercial metropolis and not an actual capital. It is not the home of its nation's political brains, nor (even with the UN) of other nation's brightest personalities. It lacks a grandly lighted stage on which society and politics, art and intellect habitually perform. It lacks the proximity of Whitehall to Pall Mall, the atmosphere of men crossing from their council chambers to their clubs. New York lacks, finally, a corresponding drawing-room life, mingling people of many cultures who represent many types of career, who exhibit many forms of talent—the ambassadorial cheek by jowl with the artistic and scientific, the man of action with the man of power and the man of thought. If the UN has brought a measure of this to New York, its tone still seems too dry, its executants mainly second violins.

However often stressed, New York's commercial character is yet impossible to ignore. For if New York has nothing of the national capital to offset its commercialism, it has too little the air of a cultural capital as well. Lincoln Center will perhaps help create this air; thus far, it seems too distinctly a "project," it seems too strenuously committed to making good. Rockefeller Center is, if anything now is, the city's center. The name—a money symbol—is itself a central one; and the thing is a vast real-estate development that throws in ice-skating to sinew the body and movies to stir the mind. Indeed, the lack of visual history in New York's existing architecture is matched by the lack of cultural history in its outward guise and air. How many New York family names symbolizing wealth and position suggest intellect or culture? * "Old New York" names, except for a few identified with early military and political careers, survive as geographical areas or telephone exchanges. Just what did the Beekmans or the Van Cortlandts *do*? To be sure, there was John Jay and, adoptively, Alexander Hamilton; and there have been the Roosevelts. As we move forward, there emerge the Astors, Vanderbilts, Morgans, who could boast of ballrooms holding only four hundred, or of inventing contract bridge, or of tyrannizing over the Metropolitan Museum. And all such names remain money names to this day; only with the Harrimans, the Lehmans, the Rockefellers—none of them at all "old" families—does money begin to suggest other interests and achievements. New York's most dynamic mayor was named La Guardia; † its best-known university president,

* Is it perhaps worth noting that Henry Adams, who had claims to all four things, lived in Boston, London and Washington—and loved San Francisco—but disliked and steered clear of New York? Henry James, a native, hated it and seldom went there; Edith Wharton left it and lived aboard.

† Thanks to Tammany Hall, New York long evoked something no less corrupt than commercial.

Nicholas Murray Butler, was best known as a frightful bully and snob. The better names, few of them very resplendent, mix Olmsted with Schurz, Nast with Riis, Hand with Isaacs, Godkin with Damrosch, Cooper with Moses. Benefactions aside, how many New York families stand for high culture today? Who, today, *are* New York's great families? Who *are* New York's living great men? If we mean public figures or men of action, aren't most of them best described as big shots?

Yet the very lack of historic culture, the strong sense of something immediate, opportunistic, ephemeral, is what makes New York in its own way overwhelming. It is not at all a museum, it is a marvelous show window. It is, again, not a history book but a crackling morning paper. New York has also a large "immigrant population" drawn from the rest of America—vast numbers of residents with no local roots. Nor is much stress put on roots; in New York one's past proves far less troubling than one's future.

The recent hordes of native immigrants have come to New York very much as foreigners once came to America —to a land of material promise. But New York's neo-immigrants are a special breed. In terms of material promise, they come to a peculiar world, a world where almost nothing material is turned out; to a New York that is not the loom or the oven or the stockpile of Business, nor its brawn or heft or hands; but its brain center, its nerve center, its voice. If, from far back, New York has given a commercial look to our culture, what it does now is bring a kind of cultural gloss to our commerce. A few manufacturing areas, like the garment district, may still exist; but New York today is the hub of cultural gimmicks, verbal gambits, promotional ploys; of all the brain children of publicity; of turning status into sales, novelty into need, marriage into bank loans, parenthood into guilt. The city's principal commodity is still money; but today Wall Street itself leans on Madison Avenue: growth stocks are endowed with semi-philosophic overtones, and Merrill, Lynch quote in their ads from Sir Francis Bacon and *Pride and Prejudice*. Indeed, the phrasemongers, the art-diluters, the thought-tenderizers fill the town (in advance of flooding the country) with facts and figures, questionnaires and surveys, slogans, stunts, testimonials, prize contests, package deals. These people are a growing New York race, important out of all proportion to their numbers—though they are numerous enough; and they at one end, as Café Society at the other, infiltrate the city's cultural life. They are prompt at its theatres, prominent at its smart restaurants and bars; they help support its art and music, they buy its books. Inquiring and adaptable, they are a great new facet of culture—appreciating it after nightfall, adulterating it during the day.

At the same time that New York has become a hub for word-mongers, it is less and less a home for writers. It remains a great book-publishing center, and magazine-publishing center, and it serves writers from all over as a hotel. Also, by virtue of their journalistic routines, many critics—of books, plays, music, art—live in or near New York. Thanks, too, to New York's academic life—to Columbia, in particular—a number of writers and book-authoring intellectuals live in Manhattan. But New York is no longer, in the true literary sense, a city of writers. It is not just that the Village has become a honky-tonk: it is that fewer and fewer, shall we say creative writers, live *anywhere* in Manhattan.

For some of this, to be sure, there are good reasons: teaching jobs throughout the country, or the desire for a quieter life, or the high cost of Manhattan living. But, while granting often valid enough causes, at the moment I would speak of the effect. Except for perhaps the very young, there is no longer about New York any sense of the one right place for writers, any sense of *milieu*. There is no special restaurant, no special rendezvous, as once the Algonquin or even the Lafayette was; or as, say, Sardi's is for theatre people today. And there is no longer the old yeast and savor and, on occasion, champagne of literary intermingling. Even Prohibition, which made for bad liquor and rowdiness, even radicalism, which made for bad literature and wrangling, gave New York a genuine writers' world. At a highbrow level today, literary parties are often *too* literary, which means they aren't parties. They are rife with half-pedagogical discussion, but are little aerated by bright talk. They run largely to professors, to critics, to intellectuals who are marginal writers, and the atmosphere is over-academic—something befitting a faculty lunch table, but not very gay after dark. Most of the men present seem unaware that there are things one does not discuss before ladies—gritty magazine controversies, for example, or post-

Existentialist thought. At lower levels, the parties are more genial but often too journalistic; the anecdotes are better but the careerism is more pronounced, or Café Society too much in evidence. Despite notable exceptions, something at once socially ingrained and ebulliently impromptu has vanished from literary parties. You get quite as much ego as formerly, but far less temperament; probably as much alcohol—and perhaps as much acid— but little festive froth.

Whose witty remarks, these days, circle the town? What women have glamour, how many hostesses any cachet? Who among the guests have brilliant dash, or even a wacky charm? If my questions seem right out of a Sunday-supplement article, and smack of parody, it is all the same the answers that must bear the burden of proof. Elinor Wylie and Edna Millay, Robert Benchley and Dorothy Parker, Muriel Draper and Mabel Dodge, Hart Crane and Dylan Thomas, Scott Fitzgerald and Thomas Wolfe—I don't know that a literary world is the better for being bohemian or bacchanalian or glamorous; but when full of people who are not only dry biscuits at parties, but also lack flavor in print, it scarcely accords with a great cosmopolitan capital.

And from a cultural standpoint, the city itself is fast losing its color. This is in part from ruthlessly killing it off, from being so overt and strident in its procedures as no longer to be evocative; so price-tag conscious, so *dernier-cri* fickle, so herdedly chic, as to leave no opportunity—or even time-interval—for patina. The Plaza and the Algonquin are the only hotels left with a glint of the past. The Waldorf suggests dinners for two thousand people; New York's public schools and branch libraries, its small parks and great squares are almost all seedy-looking or downright shabby. Broadway, the most famous thoroughfare in the Western Hemisphere, has nowhere, for even a few blocks, either real looks or character. And air-conditioning has become a Manhattan necessity as much to keep out noise as to combat heat.

If New York yet remains a great city, as opposed to just a very big one, it is in part from having the qualities of its defects, and in greater part from what, by way of people and things, it has supremely. "Things" can mean material things—more and better shops, or restaurants, or hotels. But their crucial superiority lies in cultural institutions and events, in New York's museums and concert halls, theatres and opera and ballet; its array of conductors, directors, performers, whether resident or visiting, annual or occasional, long-term or overnight. All Americans make their real artistic reputation by way of New York; all foreign celebrities at length cash in on it there. The sum total permits superb participation in all the arts.

New York has an equal primacy with people. Despite being no such true capital as London or Paris, in one way or another it is unmatched in its hemisphere for superior human beings. Beyond all the visitors, there are the residents associated with the arts; or with great institutions—whether museums or libraries, law schools or architectural firms; the experts and specialists, whether biologists or surgeons, Orientalists or city planners. Add to these, men of wide general culture; of action and thought; men who control things, create things, keep things in motion, and New York—however parochial particular atmospheres, however provincial particular lives—has large, unlocal, unobstructed perspectives. Here, the sum total permits superb participation in human beings.

In actual practice, to be sure, one's participation may be rather less than superb. It costs a lot of money, it needs a lot of pull, it presupposes a lot of leisure, to enjoy all New York's first rate cultural events; while to know lots of distinguished inhabitants and meet lots of distinguished visitors, one would have to be fairly distinguished—or unusually fortunate—oneself. But, in a relative sense, the point still holds good. Though few of us have the means to enjoy high culture *en bloc*, or the standing to meet illustrious people *en masse*, in New York as nowhere else we can all choose from an imposing menu of events, an enticing roster of personalities. The effect can be doubly tonic. Beyond the pleasure it can provide, there is the real challenge it imposes—the need, among people at least as good as yourself, to hold your own. You bumble, you bluff, you pontificate at your peril. "Nothing is so intolerable," said Chekhov, "as a provincial celebrity." New York has its sufficiently intolerable celebrities, but they are not provincial, and very few of them are enshrined. New York, after all, has the largest lion house in the world.

Nor, whether for good reasons or bad, is New York itself provincial. Its dearth of civic traditions, its general lack of roots, its constant flow of people—all this makes it too shifting and unsorted for any strong local point of view, for any true point of view at all. It is less a climate than a barometer. It has few shibboleths or social laws; it leaves you free, if only from indifference or forgetfulness. What actually helps to make it so unprovincial is its being so cheerfully parochial, a succession of city-sized villages based on economic levels, social standards, racial backgrounds, religious ties: these give it distinct neighborhood characteristics and tastes. But, as against the sprawling, widely separated equivalents in most great cities, New York can squeeze half a dozen huge villages into three or four miles. And thanks to such metropolitan compactness, the village life has a peculiar charm, giving one a local habitation but no sense of feeling cramped: in five minutes you can cross a frontier. Furthermore, the village life imposes almost no obligations or protocol. It gives you the particular kind of shops and services— and atmosphere—you want, while letting you off any social life you don't. Pleasantly villagy, New York is not at all suburban. You can live in your village for years and not have to join anything, turn up anywhere, or go with anybody.

There yet remains, as I said at the outset, the fact that New York can make its residents dissatisfied with other American cities rather than enamored of itself. And it does often indicate a negative preference rather than a positive devotion or delight. But this is not wholly an indictment, for what can be positive about civic devotion may be worse even than provincial, may be undiscriminating and chauvinist. The fact that so many New Yorkers have no local roots, no lineaged stake, no sentimental ties may help explain their wholly empirical, their thoroughly *realistic* preference for it. Sometimes such realism may point to their careerist presence in it. But if on careerist terms New York breeds a hateful, destructive competitiveness, on social and intellectual ones it stresses standards, it demolishes complacency. And if the danger of contamination is greater in New York, the *nature* of its contamination is less insidious, less deceiving—it is plainly vulgar and corrupt, not petrified and genteel. In the end, a man of some fibre will succumb to less in New York than in superficially more decorous places, because there is less to lull his vigilance, to stroke his vanity; less that proves compensating, less that consoles. New York is not a place of refuge or reassurance, though perhaps as good a place to forget in as to be forgotten.

◈◈◈◈◈◈◈◈◈◈◈

Unbrave New World

It was not so long ago that one associated pills with a sickroom, or a doctor, or at least some semblance of disease. True enough, one could be up and about when one took them—very likely, Father took a pill before meals for his dyspepsia; or Mother one before going to bed for her fluttery heart. But they were well on in life; and the pills, beyond being prescribed for ailments, were indications of age. They went with giving up tennis, and going on diets, and needing bifocals. At the very least, they were portents that the night cometh; and far oftener, they were direct evidence that the doctor had just gone away.

The pill of today, however, is something that has spectacularly come up in the world; or, to be more accurate, that now goes regularly out into it. The pill has become as much a part of a young matron's handbag as the lipstick, and rather more a part of a young executive's coat pocket than a cigarette case. And one reaches, indeed, for a pill very much as one reaches for a cigarette. It eases the moment. One turns to a pill, again, very much as one turns to a drink; it relaxes the nerves. One takes a pill after brushing one's teeth in the morning—as a stimulant. One takes a pill after brushing one's teeth at night—as a sedative. The fact is, one just takes pills. Each, after the fashion of Ecclesiastes, has its purpose and its function—a pill to sleep and a pill to wake; a pill to induce dreams and a pill to banish them; a pill before seeing a client and two pills before lunch with the boss.

Nor does the value of pills stop with their seeing people through a particular situation—with making them shyer or more truculent, sweeter or more intimidating. Pills not only relax conversationalists, they stimulate conversation. "What tranquillizer do you use?" will soon be as common coin as "What paper do you read?" or "What bridge system do you follow?" One swaps tranquillizers, like recipes. One samples them, like mints. One grades them, like vintage wines. And one doesn't merely say of one's tranquillizer: "I've got some on me, if you'd like to try one"; one says equally: "I've got one in me, if you'd care to observe the results."

The complete pill trousseau, which is very extensive indeed, has come to exist, of course, in the wake of Freud and in the wake of war, in the heyday of an exhausting cocktail culture, and at the high noon of man's new pressure-cooker style of living. Surely it is not surprising —with the unquietness of the present and the terrors of the future; the aggressions men exhibit and the guilt they conceal—that, in view of all this, people should so much desire these courage-givers and fear-relaxers, these rain makers and sun lamps of the psyche and the ego. No wonder pills have come to act as people's chauffeurs and masseurs and personal maids, as their governesses and cheerleaders and sparring partners, since without one kind of pill people are noticeably less amiable, and without another kind decidedly less coherent, and without a third kind glaringly less alive. Each pill has its special duties, like a well-trained servant in an amply staffed house. And by virtue of them, people, during short performances in almost any role, can successfully stage-light and stage-manage their destinies. Medicine evokes all the strange sudden marvels of magic under the rational auspices of Science; and the medicine chest regulates our rooms.

The question does arise, to be sure, whether having ourselves so flawlessly under control, we have ourselves —in a different sense—under any control at all; and even whether we may not have exchanged a vital part of ourselves for what we carry in our handbags and our coat pockets. In all this I hope I shall not be misunderstood. I don't mean to revive all the arguments that are as ancient as the first blind spluttering attacks on the Machine Age, wherein Science was the implacable enemy, on the one hand of Faith, and on the other hand of Art; arguments which held that anything mass-consumed furthered the cause of conformity; or which claimed, in an era of capitalist expansion, that rapacity was the mother of invention. On the contrary, it seems to me that no one can be a genuine humanist who has not a sound appreciation of the uses of the machine and the increasing wonders of Science; for he alone really understands where they do and where they do not apply.

Still less do I mean to ignore, or minimize, the conditions under which almost all people live today. Ours is an age of incessant anxiety; and our vivid awareness of the fact is scarcely calculated to make us less anxious. Ours, all too graphically, is an age of violence; and being reminded of the fact at every turn is hardly calculated to make us less scared. If happy nations have no history, doubtless happy ages have no headlines; and this is an age of staggering headlines, the least calamitious of them concerning an occasional Mad Bomber among all the sane ones. Inevitably, there must be an endless need for help; a demand for signposts and a cry for answers.

What is evident in this groping for certainties, this following all sorts of prescriptions, this needing so many real and symbolic pills, is that people have everywhere become *dependents*. They are living off someone else's answers very much in the spirit of living off someone's alms. They are having all their little daily problems cut up into little pieces for them the way their nurses and mothers used to cut up their meat. It seems to me bad enough that, as conformists, so many people should borrow their standards; or that, as disciples, so many other people should borrow their tastes. Doubtless public opinion has always had a tremendous bearing on private success. Doubtless, too, there will always be rabid disciples subscribing exultantly to exacting disciplines. But during

very few ages, I would think, have so many people led
lives of so much exhaustion and so little adventurousness;
embraced such stodgy and unimpassioned gospels,
quested such worldly and unperilous goals. Nor do I refer
only to the good gray professions, or Madison Avenue, or
Hollywood Boulevard. I mean, too, the intellectuals, or
the would-be intellectuals, or the would-have-been intellectuals. I mean the bright young men who are swallowing each and every one of the New Criticism's pills, and
always with the ashen look of patients who have been told
that, if they don't follow exact instructions, they haven't a
year to live. The whole atmosphere of culture has become
medicinal, where it is not narcotic; and as joylessly rapt
as it is joylessly hectic. Indeed, sometimes the doctor
himself has to tell the patient to ease up a little: T. S.
Eliot, in his lecture, *The Frontiers of Criticism,* carefully
slighted the element of explanation in criticism and
pointedly stressed the element of *enjoyment,* adding that
it was the latter element that people should particularly
cultivate right now.

Indeed, beyond a lack of daring or a penchant for
differing, our age would seem to have lost all historical
sense; to have forgotten that at any given moment almost
every theory or gospel, almost every composer or painter
or poet, is either being underrated or overrated. Indeed,
someone has remarked that in terms of English literature
over the last century or so, Shakespeare and Jane Austen
alone have not at some time been under a cloud. But the
stresses of the moment have largely obliterated the perspective of the centuries; the craving for answers has

sadly blurred the fact that no answers can be absolute
and not very many can be lasting; that one generation's
Magellan is another's Cook's Tourist, that one generation's Pasteur is the next generation's spreader of germs.

Most depressing of all, however, in people's becoming
such a race of dependents in that even their *self*-knowl-
edge is being wholly acquired from without. Up to a
point, outside help is indispensable—whether through
the accumulated wisdom of the world's thinkers, or
through the special insights of psychiatry and medicine.
But in our present passion for specialists and craving
for answers, we judge (and acquit or convict) ourselves,
we examine (and restrain or rouse) ourselves, we dramatize (and lash or caress) ourselves more in terms of
other men's formulas than of our own personal findings.
We are this year's most stylish model of man, in match-
ing colors; or we are drawing-book outlines in which we
are permitted to do a little personal crayoning of our
own. We can be truly grateful for keys that open various
doors to self-understanding; but we should be a trifle
leery of master keys, of packaged answers, of universal
solutions.

The large answers have, as a rule, great validity in
terms of entire human continents; but every man is, indeed, an island—and there is another meaning to the
phrase than that which Donne intended or Hemingway
made famous. For islands, however much they may need
or have in common with the mainland, have much too
that is peculiar to themselves. They have exposed positions and vexing weathers and treacherous waters all

their own; and only by taking their own soundings, and consulting their own barometers, and studying their own vegetation, only through something inwardly and locally arrived at, can each human island survive, let alone thrive and prosper.

What surely is one of the comic, and yet not too comic, phenomena of our age is that a great maxim of personal responsibility and mature achievement—Do It Yourself—is now the enthroned cliché for being occupied with nonessentials. Do It Yourself now applies to painting the porch or calking the boat, to making a screen out of oddments found in the attic, or a henhouse out of packages that arrive in the mail. On the other hand, for smoothing out a ruffled ego or solving a moral dilemma, Do It Yourself is adjudged the most primordial imbecility. It is restricted to what you can do with your hands, arms, possibly feet and conceivably shoulders. It is socially bad form, as well as morally presumptuous, for anything you do with your mind or your heart. For such matters, we turn to a book or lie down on a couch, when indeed we do not take to our bed; and the method frequently has good results. But, besides making every small situation a crisis, it *is* habit forming; it does turn us into dependents. We might try, for a change, becoming our own authorities. There is a story about Thomas Hardy using the word "smalling" while writing something, and then wondering whether there was any literary warrant for the word. So he went to the big Oxford Dictionary and found that one well-known writer had used it previously: Thomas Hardy.

Seeking answers in too external and dependent a way would not be so bad if it were true and toughly honest answers that we sought. But many people today don't want honest answers insofar as honest means unpleasant or disturbing. They want a soft answer that turneth away anxiety. They want answers that are, in effect, escapes. They want the blinds pulled down, rather than up, on reality. Max Plowman once said relevantly that Victorian poetic ideas pursued not "truth, but comfort"; and in a sense much exceeding Cardinal Newman's description of Christianity as a religion of consolation, some of today's resurgent religiousness would seem actuated less by faith than fear.

All too much of our cultural, as well as of our physical, quest is for tranquillizers. Even some of the more austere intellectual dogmas of the moment are only tranquillizers with a bitter taste; for what, in a way, can tranquillize better than their gospel of certainties, their touchstones succinctly distinguishing all good from bad, all sheep from goats, and disallowing that sheep may have goat's blood on the mother's side? The dogmas tranquillize, too, by denying the need—and discouraging the inclination—of the disciple to decide for himself. Even, I think, an excessive interest in such matters as symbolism and myth must be tranquillizing; does not the persistent need to see one thing in terms of another argue a certain disinclination to see things as they are? It is one thing to dig, but another to live underground.

In the theatre, which shows the greatest cultural lag among the arts and is liable, from the way it operates, to the greatest cultural corruption, it is particularly easy to watch audiences being handed their tranquillizers. For the theatre, by reason of its try-out tour, constantly dirties its clean linen in public, constantly revises and softens and sweetens in New Haven or Boston so that New York can be sufficiently soothed. It is possible sometimes, even from one night to the next, to see a play that began as realism caramelized into romance, or one that started off as drama bleached by successive washings into comedy. (A correspondent queried a review I wrote of the Broadway production of *A Hole in the Head*, in which I spoke of an unpleasant uncle who, all too pleasantly at the end, came through with a needed check. "At the original opening in Wilmington," my correspondent told me, "uncle resolutely declined to write out a check.")

We all want what, since it is an eighteenth-century title, the century must have wanted also: Pills to Purge Melancholy; and master keys to everything but Bluebeard's Closet; and rousing second-act curtains but reassuring third-act ones. We all *want* the world neatly divided into sheep and goats—it makes things so much easier. And if we vote Yes for Verdi, then No for Wagner; and if Yes for Art, then No for Science; and on that basis historical perspectives can be as disconcerting as personal dilemmas. For where are the truths, or even the slaves, of yesteryear? "Who now reads Bolingbroke?" asked Burke. Who now calls for leeches, or even gluten bread, or remembers Dalcroze, or follows Montessori?

In the face of all this, one could hardly have a specific solution of one's own to offer; but one can offer sympathy. Life for most of us is full of steep stairs to go puffing up and, later, of shaky stairs to totter down; and very early in the history of stairs must have come the invention of banisters. Let us all make use of banisters, and wherever possible, of elevators. All the same, I fear that man is born for trouble as the sparks fly upward; and trouble probably won't vanish even when Science succeeds—and it will—in making sparks fly down. It is one of the great glories of Science, but one of its great inconveniences also, that it discredits and invalidates and proves false as often as it corroborates and certifies and proves true. Since, despite our master keys, Time keeps rusting the locks on all our doors, and since for every Alexander the Great there are a dozen Ozymandiases, we might think of changing our regimens and of living morally and intellectually *à la carte* for a while. We might sample poets and painters, attitudes and opinions, that are not featured on the menu. We might try to be relativists about a world that is really not less beautiful for being half-clouded and half-starry. "Joyous distrust," said Nietzsche, "is a sign of health. Everything absolute belongs to pathology."

·III·

◇◈◇◈◇◈◇◈◇◈◇◈◇

Reflections and Complaints

of Late Middle Age

I WAS ABOUT to say that, as opposed to things like one's judgment and taste, one is not pretentious about one's age—only to suspect that about one's age one may be most pretentious of all. One's late middle age, at least; for, together with all the sighs and self-pity for having come so far along life's way, goes vast self-satisfaction for *having* come so far—and recently with Wisdom as a traveling companion. Wisdom of a sort, to be sure: perhaps not the philosopher's wisdom, those eyeglasses that are never quite right for one's eyes; nor the mystic's, those eyes gazing inward and upward, but never around and about; but his who has indeed often blundered, been an ass at times, and a nuisance, and a bore, but by now has come to profit by it all. Oh *he,* more than ever, remarks that man's vanity and stupidity

are eternal; more than ever, now he is fifty-nine, mur-
murs that the mule in us, and the ostrich, and the pea-
cock, grow only more pronounced. But to know all this
and freely confess it; and sit watching others rush
busily about, saving the world, and discovering the
obvious, and confiding the proverbial; and to find now
even the freshest words an echo, the boldest thoughts a
plagiarism,—surely this is to have come far, and grown
uncommonly mellow.

Alas, about late middle age one can't even for long be
self-mocking. Any fun in the first paragraph only makes
for trouble in the second. With every writer near sixty
the backward glance must be peculiarly compulsive,
whether for things to hurry past or linger over; but
more acceptable than any glance forward. For after
sixty one's future must be spent in a foreign land; there
is little one can take culturally, socially, even humanly
for granted; can merely allude to, can leave unsaid. This
is not true, to be sure, in small picturesque ways, in
telling the young about the slang or popular songs, the
speakeasies or literary hangouts, of the '20s: about such
things they will often be glad to hear. And I don't really
mean in terms of future esthetic tastes, or fashions in
art and letters. These may jolt what one takes for
granted, but then one has always taken it for granted
that they would; has always known that art and letters
wait for no man, and that the time would come when
one called some young man's music a yawp, and some
young man's paintings a daub, and some young man's
writing a screed. What seem a real assault on what

middle age has taken for granted are fifty little breaches of manners—a nice way of saying No, perhaps; or an engaging way of saying "I'm sorry." Or fifty small mutations of behavior, or in misbehavior. Or what passes for morality, or is permissible immorality. This last, perhaps, most of all: as one nears sixty, there is nothing one feels so sure about as what constitutes decent and acceptable sin.

And as one moves around at that age—and overhears, or hears wrong; and notices or can't quite see; and talks to people and is suddenly addressing the air—each uncertain reaction begets a disquieting thought. What, one wonders—clutching at least at a *phrase* that is new— what is the public image of me? Academic fossil? Club bore? Do people laugh at me behind fans? Do they hide from me behind pillars? Do they think of me as I once thought of—well, Henry Seidel Canby?

Fortunately, as one side of oneself turns touchy, another remains splendidly immune. It is not just that one's private image of oneself may suggest an *eminence grise*. More realistically, one goes back to where one started: this is being sixty-ish, and grown too much the praiser of past times from being the prisoner; and aware that as the arteries harden, the memories turn soft; and that, as one's age takes shape, one's personal astronomy alters. Once oneself was the planet, and life the sun it revolved around; now, being pre-everything, even pre-Copernican, it is life that circles oneself. That modest fundamental accepted, one can very happily keep going, even going forward; can shrug that the road leads downhill, or that the topography is so foreign and so flat. What one does, indeed, is to acquire a very helpful *tourist's* psychology. What one does is look on all small breaches of manners as quaint; all misbehavior as exotic; all offensive morality as primitive. This leads to something more helpful still. One now regards the cultural life one encounters, as not something later than one's own, but earlier. Hence there is no need to croak about how decadent the times are, or how effete the young: one can mutter instead how crude they are, and even ape-like; one can emerge no elderly, headshaking scold, but a mature, observant, detached anthropologist. One no longer wants, say, 1964's cars to revert to 1926's—one wonders how long till they can catch up with them. One no longer wants to go back from the fifteenth edition of the *Britannica* to the eleventh; one hopes civilization will ultimately reach it. Just when, one asks, will the jet achieve the finality of the 20th Century Limited? How many years must it take for TV to become radio, and then for radio to become the morning paper?

Meanwhile, fascinated by the quaint, the exotic, the primitive, one gazes at various specimens, one peers into corners, one squints through binoculars. Eventually, having examined everything and noted the effect on the natives, one proceeds to pass judgment. Cannibalism, one announces, is more than a dubious practice, it is a very monotonous diet. Installing in one's own bed the wife of the couple who seek a night's lodging, while assigning the husband a straw pallet on the floor, is questionable hospitality. To turn anthropologist at 59 may seem hazardous, but can be very exhilarating. It is also full-blooded and virile—no querulous letters to the papers, no prissy grumbling at the club. Instead of writing rather irritable memoirs, one assembles a great many ego-warming case histories.

· 2 ·

Actually, except for an increasing need to keep in physical repair, late middle age isn't a bad one at all. It conduces to a kind of enlightened self-absorption, which is to say having the ego always about one, but on leash. The shift to pre-Copernican astronomy is true enough, but then it embraces a pre-Copernican cosmos.* One has made oneself the center; but the center of a rather small, rather coordinated world. For the man of culture—I don't say for the man of action—late middle age means a lessened will to power, an ironic if not yet extinct ambitiousness. Oh, deep down things may churn and seethe and rage, and it would perhaps take very little to make vast ambitions stir. But the moment has, I think, arrived when self-knowledge, which isn't too hard to come by, can hope to merge with self-acceptance, which is very hard. For some time past one has been well aware that one was not Prince Hamlet, and chiefly afraid that one might be Polonius instead.

The age one has now reached oneself naturally re-

* Need I say I am speaking here of the private life; not of one's concern for contemporary problems?

coils from the age one now inhabits. What alone miti-
gates the horror the nuclear world arouses, or the sense
of responsibility it entails, is that it most of all arouses a
sense of helplessness. How little oneself can do, and how
much any reckless fool or villain. Besides, what a ter-
rible two-edged sword is *morality*—what a ruthless, because self-righteous, weapon. I am more moral than you,
my cause is more moral than yours, my Father in Heaven
can lick your Father in Heaven. Men have perhaps
oftener died for slogans than for bread, for God than
for Mammon, and if history teaches us anything it is
that fanaticism has made more blood flow than villainy.

· 3 ·

As for writing my memoirs, I've never given it serious thought; with anything beyond the anecdotal I would
be too uneasy. It seems quite enough, by trying to formulate a view of the world around one, to suggest one's
own. What one finds right and wrong with existence
may well convey what is right and wrong with oneself.
Besides, I've kept no diaries and can no longer remember what I imagined life, or my life, might be. Whatever
the answer for either, I proposed at nineteen to find it
in New York; and going there in the mid-1920s, came
upon something at least unruly enough to seem rebel-
lious, untidy enough to seem bohemian, unfamiliar
enough to seem superior. All this, linked to something
genuinely literary, could make even a young man who
kept to the shallow end of the pool feel its buoyancy

and swell. Even for those who had no vast belief in themselves, the '20s were invigorating, because life was so uncautious and confident, literature so confident and uncramped. And if radicalism or even liberalism was then no battle cry, one could perhaps be negative about issues from something so affirmative in life. And one was satiric and skeptical because such an attitude had a great tradition behind it—of wit, élan, urbanity.

The '30s appeared, bluntly declarative—the wolf at the door, the handwriting on the wall. They sobered me but they didn't really suit me. This, I think, arose less from how uneasily I fell in with their politics than from my not being political-minded at all. My moral sense, my humanitarian impulses, my half-anarchist protesting-ness often responded; but in part from temperamental unfitness, in part from intellectual limitations, I re-mained at heart an outsider. What, with me, made for doubts was how, in this grim sober 1930's world, one had always to get intellectually a little tipsy to respond to it, where for all the bootleg blur of the '20s, one's mind seemed effortlessly one's own. The '30s were tre-mendous in outline—for some a tragic or heroic experi-ence; for others, a too black-and-white melodrama; for every aware person, a problem—whether of sustenance or of survival; of allegiance or of revolt. The '30s were remarkable enough to bring every one back to his senses, while in some degree taking leave of them. Their sombre, or their stage-lighted, side encouraged every one to as-sume some kind of role, if only in retrospect. But where the '20s had flattered my desire to be dashing and bold, and gave me—if only as Walter Mitty—a great feeling of participation, the '30s constituted a valuable—but an academically, not personally, valuable—experience. They revealed what life itself could be: not simply a Depression reality, or even a totalitarian one; indeed not so much a reality as a realization—a realization that evil truly exists on a large scale; that the thirst for power is as fierce as the facts of it are brutal; that ruthlessness can lurk behind a slogan, and treachery maneuvre inside a cause. The realization did not wipe out one's sense of how much in human nature can be courageous and devoted, but it did make clear how Fascism and Communism can exploit what is starved and sick and warped and bitter—and sometimes beastly—in it.

I was forty when World War II ended, and I suppose for the most part "formed." That may explain why subsequent eras have struck me as so formless. Doubtless too, the '20s and '30s left too vivid an impress. But if there has seemed, since World War II, less sense of pattern, there has been far greater awareness of change. The change is, of course, exactly what *youth* takes for granted. If, say, the '20s doggedly refused to be shocked, the '60s scarcely have it in them to be surprised, certainly on any physical or mechanical basis. The Atomic Age has made "impossible" an anachronism. Time has become its plaything, Space its major sport; and now that a man can say to his wife, "Well, if you're playing bridge this afternoon, I think I'll circle the globe," the imagination has turned pauper, and the wildest boast an understatement. In any case, the quarter-century that has not just introduced but made part of our lives—to name but a few things—aeronauts and H-bombs, TV, air-conditioning, antibiotics, motels, super-highways, drip-dry, deep-freezes, is without parallel, not for what it forecasts but for how it demolishes forecasting. Doubtless every generation, had it awakened from a thirty-year sleep, would have found remarkable surprises, but almost always as extensions of what it had known. Even thirty years ago, one pictured the future in terms of food pellets, or 200-story skyscrapers, or living to well over a hundred. We little guessed the power of TV to enslave society, or the power of aeronautics to conquer space, or the power of bombs to annihilate continents. Yet no single aeronaut—perhaps because the first to triumph was a Russian—could give Americans, in circling the globe, quite the kind of thrill that Lindbergh did by crossing the Atlantic. The reason, clearly, is that for young people today things move so *fast* there is no problem of adjustment. Before you can adjust to A, B has appeared leading C by the hand, and with D in the distance.

The old sense of permanence, which often made people short-sightedly resistant to change, has gone. Gone even with the very young. For however much, in other days, the very young cried out for change or shouted for progress, they always visualized, however mistakenly, their own future. They would also, quite unconsciously, preserve from the *status quo* anything they found desirable. Today's generation cannot; things happen and change too fast for it to formulate a future, prove too menacing for it to be sure of one. The sense of global uncertainty has rather bred a great wish for local security, an impulse to settle for a bit of the limelight and not seek a place in the sun. But I don't think it is so much the menace of the future that destroys a feeling for permanence, as the character of the present. To-day's mechanical mutability—the way things are so quickly out-of-date and shelved and discarded; are never streamlined or time-saving or drip-dry *enough;* are never convertible or interchangeable or reversible enough—has killed the feeling for permanent modes of living, and of behavior and belief scarcely less. Constantly trading-in cars, constantly tossing out furniture, moving from town to suburb, from basement-with-garden to penthouse-with-terrace, from Baltimore to Sweden, switching from one social and even ethnic group to another, shifting children from one kind of school to another, never having even a dentist one can call one's own—here, surely, is all the rapidity of the jet combined with all the root-lessness of the trailer.

Permanent values, settled beliefs, social traditions grow less and less easy. With the present as well as the future unstabilized, there emerges a sort of tourist be-havior, of trial-subscription morality. "When in Rome . . ." becomes the norm, for one is forever in Rome, in temporary quarters, in transit, whether of geography or income, social attitudes or cultural assumptions. And along with being forever on the move, one is forever in a hurry, leaving things inadvertently behind—friend or fishing tackle, old raincoat or old allegiance. As for the journey into the future, everything is subject to change without notice, and not just "The 10.31 to Harrisburg has been discontinued" but "Trains have been discontinued."

What complicates all this is that while nothing lasts long enough to be sacred, for as long as it lasts everything is *de rigueur*. In all this vast atmosphere of change, personal development, private morality, individual experiment don't float free; they are all manacled to Public Opinion. Tossing out the furniture, shifting the terrain, never means that permanence is felt to be petrefaction, or settledness, parochialism. In all this change there is no break with anything bourgeois, no distrust of tradition, no faith in experiment. In other words, there is no *choosing* of flux on philosophical grounds, as a way of life; or on temperamental grounds, as a form of dissent; or on intellectual grounds, as a means of inquiry. Never have so many people led a gypsy's life with so much of a joiner's psychology.

Whatever one's middle-aged dissatisfaction with all this, the basis for it is too explicable to ignore, the result too understandable to indict. One cannot but see what the speed of mechanical progress has done to shape the present, even without regard to how nuclear energy may overshadow the future. *My* sense of frantic speed has become the normal pace—the young men in a hurry go not by twos or threes but by hundreds along the street. In a corporation-run society, it grows as futile to preach self-determination as in a TV culture to bid the airwaves stand still. But if an appeal to values can only be fruitless, there must still be some point in an appeal to horse-sense. Surely, the less one is cheered up by the portents, the more one must face up to the facts. One, even while trying to help, can feel helpless about the state of the world; but need one, quite, about one's own situation? Never, it seems to me, has helplessness been proclaimed on so grandiosely determinist a basis as today—as though there were no turns-off whatever from Madison Avenue, no exits anywhere from corporation skyscrapers; never such an air of *Ich kann nicht anders,* as though the issue were not capitulation but heresy. Never, either, has helplessness had such doubtful origins. These bright, up-and-coming people aren't victims of poverty, and so must take any job they can get; nor of discrimination, and so must take what few jobs are open to them; nor of little schooling, and so are not fitted for much; nor of a single skill, and so are fitted for one thing only; nor, like ball players, of short-term careers, and so must cash in while they can. This race of intelligent, college-bred young men, groomed for the business or professional world, do indeed have their way to make, and often no very congenial way to make it. Even when they are given a choice, it may in essence be Hobson's choice—one agency or corporation as against another, one TV system or magazine empire. If no treadmill, it can clearly become a trap. Yet its early stages need be neither ignominious nor fatal; all early stages inculcate adjustment, confer experience, count as education. "Reasonable" ambitiousness is surely valid, though its exact limits are rather harder to define. But even if we admit that today's ambitiousness is a willy-nilly thing, with half its aggressions defensive and half its impulsions born of fear, must we accept its implied alternative of Submit or Starve? If there is a real element of economic determinism involved, is there not also one of self-nutured psychology—of a whole generation accepting the set-up as doctrinal, and first capitulating to its terms and finally subscribing to its tenets? The thrust of ambition is, and always has been, great, but among the bright-eyed it had once a more adventurous and individualistic air, a much more bracing rivalry. Such rivalry seldom meant a faceless competition; as there was something more invigorating about it, there was something self-chosen, too, and self-propelled. Today's competitiveness, so much imposed from without, is exhausting, not exhilarating; is unending—a part of one's social life, one's solitude, one's sleep, one's sleeplessness.

Moreover, what emerges from it all is a new and fearful kind of risk. It is no longer whether—to be wholly realistic about it—one is willing to mortgage oneself for a period of time; or in limited degree to sell oneself for good and all. It is whether one is willing spiritually, mentally, all too often physically, to kill oneself. The rewards can be large; but the stakes are sucker stakes. They come down, not to either-or, not to all-or-nothing, not to success-or-suicide; *at best* they come down to both. Their goal is equally their epitaph: Tomb at the Top. To read in *Fortune* Magazine of life in Bloomfield Hills, Michigan, of automobile executives of varying and growing and shrinking and collapsing importance—life all five-car panic, living all gilded spikes, every neighbor a probable threat, every decision a possible death-warrant—is to encounter a form of life imprisonment commutable to death. If I make melodrama of it, it is because the executives themselves, and so many like them, cannot even give it the rousingness of melodrama, the roulette-table tingle of ruinous stakes. It all remains affluently suburban, nothing that flares into excoriating anger; never man tugging at his hateful bonds, only man swallowing his poisoned drink. Even from within it seems governed by caution and conventionality, the men too tired for selfhood, the women too timid. They have all become the cars they live by, with an outsider decreeing the speed they shall run at, and the moment to junk them.

Perhaps, though I am not at all sure, this is an extreme situation; but hundreds of others seem sufficiently typical—and insufficiently foreordained. Surely too many people have confused danger with doom; worse, far from heeding the storm warnings, have decided they decreed shipwreck. Let us allow that one knowingly, out of something like necessity, makes his Hobson's choice, elects its kind of "future." Need one, having proved very capable at one's job, be thereafter resignedly, unresistantly competitive? If one becomes a really good office manager or sales manager or advertising director, will one be unquestionably pitched out just by asking to stay put? At first, perhaps, it may be frowned upon as un-American, or looked askance at as some new dodge or gimmick. But surely in time it must be seen to make sense; given enough time, for that matter, it might start a fashion or a modest revolution. It is true, that to achieve such an end, people would have to do more than just hold venality at arm's length. They would have to master their vanity (and their wives' vanity) as well, and beyond crying "To hell with how other people live!" say "*Let* people think this was as far as I could get!"

What would be truly comic about so fierce a competition were it not ulcerating and sad, is how many of its contestants so dutifully—rather than desperately—enroll; are conformists even in ambitiousness; are not victims of any grand economic iron law, but have put themselves in an iron lung known as keeping up with the Joneses. Only, what was once suburban farce now threatens to become national tragedy. But since Keeping Up no longer applies to Babbittarian businessmen with clothes-horse wives and country-club aspirations, but to aware, educated, intelligent people, it can't—with them —altogether have to happen: they must in some sense be letting it. They must know they are being as much vulgarized as victimized. I don't insist they need feel ashamed of themselves, but I do think they might stop feeling sorry for themselves. To define their lot as capitulation may be somewhat too harsh, but it becomes too tolerant to call it coercion. Precedents do exist of people who refused promotions—unscathed; and for whom the end of the climb wasn't the end of the road. If, figuratively—if, literally—all Organization Men under forty making $25,000 or more a year formed their own organization and agreed to strike *against* higher wages for five years, what would happen? Or suppose they created a New Poor movement with snob appeal, making it smart to look shabby, the way dukes flaunt patched sleeves. It could be a fad of a kind, a game played in reverse, like losing chess; the status symbols worshipped *in absentia*, like *not* owning a Bentley. But simply by playing it, incomes might painlessly diminish, for expenses would rapidly dwindle. The analyst could be let go, along with the second gardener; and the second mortgage be dispensed with at the same time as the speedboat. For if Conformity itself, and not conforming to any set or particular things, is the national disease, why couldn't the game go right on, but played for "sensible" stakes? And we non-conforming, non-status-seeking, men with our intense inner life, we who snap our fingers at the fashions, now could own the drug-on-the-market, price-slashed Bentleys.

· 4 ·

Good sense is not, at the moment, a conspicuous American trait. It must once have been, for pioneers would have perished without it; nor, without it, could the nation—from the writing of the Constitution onward—have coped with its perils. To be sure, there were always in America offsets to good sense. Our immense natural resources, our century-long moving frontier—however exploitable for the hard-headed—were spurs to recklessness and extravagance. And no matter how coldblooded and unscrupulous our robber barrons and Wall Street plungers, they brought even to money-making a darkly romantic lure. They waded in plenty and wallowed in panics, till a Jay Gould almost ranked with a Jesse James. We love gambling, the Mississippi steamboat gambler is one of our glossiest period figures —though it was scarcely he who gambled. And gambling, as anything more than a pastime, does not consort with good sense. We love fads too, bouncing one on top of another; and fads do not consort with good sense. We love abracadabra, and spiritual as well as medical nostrums; we love secret societies (whose secrets are shared by millions); we love the Mrs. Eddys and the Billy Sundays, the broadjumps to health, the highjumps to Heaven; and these hardly consort with good sense. Even in our sovereign field, finance, we exhibit a naive belief in systems, when it is not an insane belief in miracles—gold bricks, wildcat stocks, Florida real estate, a market that goes up and need not come down; and these hardly consort with good sense. Most of the great American fortunes were made, of course, in the knowledge that we didn't have good sense; Barnum alone chose to proclaim what men who got far richer kept still about.

Ironically, though good sense has never governed the mass of Americans, something that could be mistaken for it has dominated their thinking; and just so, pitted our progress and hobbled our culture. As a result, a certain conception of "good sense" has come to worry the superior American. He has tended to identify good sense with mere practicality, to see it flecked with something prudential and veined with something philistine. "Good sense" smacks, for him, of our first secular Bible,

Poor Richard's Almanac. Poor Richard, moreover, isn't just strewn with penny whistles and talk of penny wise, it is shot through with How to Succeed; more distasteful even than its being a storehouse of materialist directives, it is a repository of Mammon-serving clichés. What aren't always the same clichés, but seem to be, are the titles of that whole library of virtuous self-interest, the Alger Books. And so, on and on—Samuel Smiles, Orison Sweet Marsden, Dale Carnegie, so that something like "good sense" has become associated with everything venal in American life, even in full view of how lacking in good sense a Babbitt was, or at odds with it an Aubrey Piper, or in desperate need of it a Willy Loman.

"Reason," with its appeal to the intellect and its echo of the Enlightenment, is far more cordially received by the superior American. But it surely *stands* to reason, that no conformist nation can be a sensible one; that good sense consists in judging things on their own merits, or adapting them to one's own needs. If there *is* something prudential about good sense—as in warning one when to quit, or refrain, or say No—you would gather from the way "good sense" is snubbed, that in all other respects superior people are deaf to self-interest; as you would gather that there was something cowardly about good sense, when there is oftenest something courageous. Since all philosophies stress how widespread is human folly, plainly the *un*foolish man must be the frequently dissenting one. To be sure, all sorts of low, materialistic, reactionary things are defended in the name of sense; but so, with no greater warrant, are they defended in the name of truth, liberty, morality, justice, patriotism and God. Finally, good sense is oftenest equated with playing safe (and therefore disparaged); but the very essence of good sense is the calculated risk.

Yet it is not only our American irrationalities that show how deficient we are in good sense; it is also our constant running to extremes. On our inventive and creative side, two things particularly stand out: a public, mass-minded, utilitarian achievement—our Edisons, Hollywoods, skyscraper cities, and a private, withdrawn, inward one—our Emily Dickinsons, Ryders, Walden Ponds. Set against the public-address system is the cryptic private language; forever scowling at the conformist is the crank. Our major writers can be, at times, as coarse-grained and obvious as Mark Twain, or as finespun and labyrinthine as Henry James. Our living shows the same extremes—utter escapism for our pleasures, resigned no-escapism in our jobs. Our business careers foster a sense of total bondage that governs our dinners as well as our lunches; so that when most Americans contrive to escape, escapism means a strenuous forgetfulness, something that excludes the mind; that blots out the morrow. (Even intellectuals can have an escapism of sorts, of fitting world problems into their own blueprinted worlds, of giving them added meanings but lessened immediacy, greater kinship with chess than with actual crisis.)

A like extremism makes for our serving God and Mammon both, and both at the same time. Perhaps I may be allowed here a digression, that is only partly one, on such a procedure. It seems to me a most unsatisfactory one, whether with those who practice it or with those who feel its effects. Yet, however much I deprecate it, it is not for thinking it among the worst of procedures. For rather than serve God and Mammon, we might serve Mammon alone; or serve God and the Devil; or the Devil alone. Mammon, to be sure, may seem like the Devil at times, or in his service; but *we* do not serve the Devil. Evil, whatever its spare, theological New England past or its lush, fictional Deep-South present, is not a very American thing. We are corrupted people but not a depraved one. We don't make pacts with Satan; what we do is *try* to make pacts with God. We would have Him understand what we are doing, and why we are doing it—now for the wife and kids; now for the well-fed body that can succor the thirsting soul; now for the good we can eventually do unto others. Do let us but prosper, O Lord, and we will make returns unto Thee. Nor are these just churchly returns, like tithes; it is almost as though God, rather than bearing with our activities, should help negotiate them, and get His commission. To be sure, we make pacts with others than God—with ourselves, not least; or, worshipping our country's historic push and drive, we instinctively emulate them. Sometimes, no doubt, we seek compensation for early want and poverty, or even revenge for injustice and pain. And we have something too with a vicious swagger about it, or a juvenile bravado; street-gang warfare or gangster war. But these are jungle-born and often foreign-born as well—dark twisted ways of sharing the Land of Plenty, or desperate dazed ways of shaming it.

But evil—something insulated by pride, and coldly exultant; something delighting in its own image and often existing for its own sake—we have nationally very little of. It has not, as in Europe, had almost as many reasons as centuries to corrode tired bones and possess tired bodies. At the higher reaches of our culture and thought, evil has not contrived subtle poisons and jagged refinements. I wonder, moreover, whether any nation can be imbued with evil that is dominated by public opinion. (There is evil in England because not public opinion but caste approval governs—and class resentments fester.) * We are always—and not, I think, with any gleeful, corrupt hypocrisy—seeking official approval, community acceptance, respectable forebears for what we do. Tartuffe we have scarcely heard of, but Mrs. Grundy we know very well. We *can* be what have been called the greatest of hypocrites, the wholly unconscious kind; and we are often what might be called the saddest kind, those who are hypocrites with themselves. But for polished dissimulation we have no talent; and for the vulgar version of it, the smoothie, we have a pretty good weather eye. As for a cynical, Iago-like pleasure in the game itself, we have no taste at all. Indeed, if we can't be ranked as solid citizens, we would at least misbehave as solid citizens periodically do, and as public

* Evil can develop in, say, Negroes and homosexuals because too often not public opinion but sheer public prejudice has militated against them.

opinion is indulgent toward. Cool to smoothies, public
opinion often chuckles at the smart cookie who looks like
an apple-cheeked lout; frowns on chiseling but is
amused by brass; and never disdains the genuine big
shot. With us, too, the end justifies the means—not according to Marx, but according to Mammon. If a man
steals enough to get really rich, he has stolen enough
to become, in time, entirely respectable; and the moment
he is no longer cut dead, he is warmly kowtowed to. Indeed, God and Mammon are alike revered as the biggest
of big shots. On the other hand, in any personal sense the
Devil remains a shadowy figure, in any professional
sense, a shady one.

One great reason for this is that we haven't the
Devil's self-sufficiency. He, like Evil, is a lone wolf; a
solitary gloater, not a social braggart. We, with our fear
of public opinion, can only embrace evil when it has the
safety and sanction of numbers—of the Ku Klux, say;
or when it commands the bravado of liquor; or the
warrant of self-righteousness. As playwrights of evil,
Americans are too limited in invention, in imagination;
can only smash, burn, rape, kill. A darker talent flourished in the Old World our forefathers came from;
and in the New World they came to, the aborigines, when
irked, were not always without aptitude either. But *we*
lack it; and we shun the Devil not just from having
public opinion to reckon with, but ourselves as well. We
have our own portable sense of guilt. We get to be hard
bargainers, even hardened crooks; but not hardened
sinners. What we do we must have *some* kind of reason

for—it cannot be an *acte gratuit*, or simply express the artist in evil. We too would say of *our* thievings, had we Falstaff's wit as well as his power of rationalization: "Tis my vocation, Hal; tis no sin for a man to labor in his vocation." For we don't undercut and doublecross, lie and look bland, let alone cheat or steal, for the artistic pleasure in it. But, vocation or not, we still all too often feel guilty; and just here, tend to fall back in our guilt on our second line of defense. For, beyond our entangling misalliances, behind a different sort of barbed wire, lie our ancestries and upbringings and boyhoods. In the midst of our sessions with guilt, comes a voice whispering absolution; whispering that it is less our fault than our fate—a huddle of hatreds and humiliations and envies that go far back in time.

This is a plea it is hard not to sympathize with. It involves more than fellow-feeling, than a "There but for the grace of God go I." It involves us: there *go* I—and you, too, conceivably; you too, on your knees to Mammon but no doer of evil; streaked with guilt, studded with grievances, tousled from pressures, haggard from not making money, maimed from making it. To hell, we cry, with the school bills! Damn the dentist! Screw the bank loan! Call it life today, call it the fate of man, call it Capitalism, call it Kismet: there go I, there go you. Is there perhaps one further question to ask: Need we go *all* the way? I suppose I was asking it a little while back, when I brought up the matter of sense.

Sense, in these parts, in these times, seems to me not just sadly lacking but supremely needed. As I have suggested, we always prefer an appeal to reason—the voice of reason, the life of reason, the Age of Reason have, certainly, far grander reverberations. But a certain "suspension" of reason in favor of sense is the very essence of sense. This is so little a reasonable world that it takes every last effort of reason—which is, only then, self-interest—to keep people from blowing it up. Few of us are reasonable for two hours on end, and hardly any in situations affecting their emotions. Need one be reminded of the Age of Reason in England—of how, during an era named for it, reason was constantly in eclipse, catastrophically in collapse; given to bitter feuds (born of childish trifles) and blood-stained riots (many *not* economic in origin) and bursting madhouses (which it was the fashion to visit)? Some program of reason must, indeed, control any reins of government; but surely nothing so philosophic and abstract can rescue men pleased to dub themselves rats; here sense, and only sense, may help, with a pure *argumentum ad murem*.

Sense always bids us reason with ourselves, but bids us simultaneously beware how we may rationalize instead. And sense, today, knows how seldom we *do* reason with ourselves; how often we hurry elsewhere—to couches and confessionals, to bookshops and symposiums, even to drugstores and liquor stores—for counsel. Moreover, we tend—the superior among us in particular—to give our problems not just dramatic vibrations but philosophic scope. For in this era of cultural absolutes—sheep and goats, prigs and panders, academic jargon and careerist cant—anything midway is in some sense disdained. *Mid* and *middle* have shed all that once suffused *aurea mediocritas* to share all that now infests *utter mediocrity*. As *mid-Victorian* once, so *midcult*, *middlebrow*, *middle-class*, *middle-of-the-road* today. But, along with this generally defensible artistic derogation of the middle, any phrase that suggests the temperate zone of life—ordinary human problems, recognizable social pressures, recurrent personal dilemmas— has been expunged from critical speech. Something more literary and grandiose must replace it—the human predicament, the need of commitment, the sense of engagement, the feeling of alienation; in sum, any high-sounding neologism, any abstract noun, any word preceded by moral. Is it surprising how many of us falter or grow faint? Who, up till now, had constantly to grapple with moral pantomime, and moral visibility, and moral fat,* while being simultaneously *engagé* and in need of commitment? Does no one see life as, inevitably, compromise—and thus try for the most intelligent compromise possible?

From far back, to be sure, *compromise* has carried with it a much worse taint than *sense*. To compromise virtually means to capitulate, though clearly the purpose of the one is to prevent the other. But doubtless that is just it—it is so glaringly midway, when not to be among the elect is to consign yourself to the outcasts. To any

---

* Within a week of writing this I found in one book review by so able a reviewer as Mr. Marius Bewley, "moral illumination," "moral insight and comprehension," "moral values," "morally inevitable," "moral discernment" and "the moral meaning of Anna."

mere weather-beaten survival, we now prefer a determinist doom. To be sure, *adjustment* has in some sense ousted *compromise;* but compromise is a procedure, where adjustment is a product; and on this cause-and-effect basis, were there a better sense of the one, there might be a larger amount of the other. In any case, from such ABC instances of compromise as "If I don't have to see your brother, you needn't see my aunt" or "We either go to Europe or buy a new car, but not both" we can often proceed toward making tame beasts of our intolerances, humorous butts of our ambitions, truces of our vendettas with the self or society.

Yet in today's pursuit of career, though everywhere the spectre of maladjustment hovers, the idea of sane, *self-respecting* compromise seems ignored. A tooth-and-nail competitiveness is regarded as a law of life, as punishing if you defy it as if you defer to it. Now, men certainly exist whose raging ambition is not to be argued with. And in other men it meshes with their sense of vocation and turns messianic. But for most men in this country it has become a sort of contagious disease. At the same time, it has been made into a kind of badge of masculinity—a trumpet-call, its notes rousing and exultant: forging ahead, joining the brass, leading the field, scaling the heights. And it favors the current credit system: Start climbing now and pay later. Only later does one learn the price, though clearly all around one, one can descry it.

As I have said, I'm not speaking of the madly ambitious—though in a sense they are the most sanely so, since they bring zest to the struggle and thrive off its ardors. Most others sensibly see material success as a means to an end. But they seldom sensibly calculate how much they can stomach of all they find burdensome, of all they find indecent, of all they find self-destroying. They seldom calculate just what price they can pay and still get the best of the bargain. But surely the one sound basis of calculation, of intelligent compromise, is not to *get* ahead but to come out ahead: you give up the part to preserve the whole. I say "intelligent compromise"—which means preserving, no worse than a little chipped and rubbed, one's self-respect; for one is still to end up a released prisoner, not a retired prostitute.

Intelligent compromise is at least the child of enlightened self-interest, and must bespeak not cynicism but good sense. Its realism is its best hope: can the rat race be stopped, or even slowed down, by any appeal to lofty principles, when the human race has so seldom been swayed by them? (If one is to be a little cynical, it is toward how often the high-principled life has been vitiated by ego and spiritual pride, or a self-congratulatory sense of rectitude, or a harsh censoriousness—and even malicious glee—about the lapses in other people.) Much of all this, in any case, is less morality than me, and but reinforces the awareness that in matters of conduct, of values, of belief, one's temperament is one's chief test. And, just so, one's prejudices largely cluster round other men's particular failings, one's sympathies round one's own. Thus the relativist—through rejecting absolutes as so unattainable as to make for rather pernicious idealism, or as so inflexible as to make for rather inhuman ideals—comes to appraise all systems and moralities by how supple they are as well as how sound; and to judge all codes of behavior by how much they benefit their advocates, and how little they penalize their opponents. And in rejecting absolutes, one rejects any effort toward total self-knowledge, or total banishment of self-delusion. But one can still keep, I think, to a low-calorie delusion diet. Thus, if we never *give* ourselves the benefit of the doubt, we may possibly be entitled to it. Thus, when the question of our motives proves troubling, let us regard it also as the answer. Good sense does not insist that we must compromise with *ourselves,* or must soliloquize on the same terms with which we must face society.

At the same time, sense urges that in soliloquy we need not dramatize, indeed universalize, the nature of everything that besets us; and thus, by exalting the predicament, double the peril. Indeed, the more imaginative, ambivalent, intellectual we are concerning our ills, the more downright and hard-headed had better be our approach. The vexed arithmetic of half our troubles may well be tied to the world's grim economics; but our therapy lies in a mastery of purely personal profit and loss. The ulcer that threatens or already torments us may well have its origins in the rank cancers of society; but prevention or cure most rests on the proper treatment for ulcers. Could it be that some of us look intellectually down our noses at blunt truths from a fear of looking straight out at them? Is it irrelevant to remember that, in the high-powered world we endlessly discuss, infinitely fewer people die in poorhouses than in madhouses—and that there seems no absolute need to die in either? Is it pointless to reflect that to have three cars at forty isn't worth what even status-worship still restricts to one hearse at 43? Though conceivably three hearses are worth a thought. In this age of sick humor, they could constitute a kind of mortuary three-card monte, with spirited bidding on which hearse holds the corpse.

· 5 ·

Sense tugs at my sleeve here, bidding me cease its praises on this playful note. Playfulness itself, at any rate, is something to include among these reflections, as a quality in sad decline, perhaps almost at the point of death. Even my three-hearses joke, if I may use it for comment, may exhibit more than a trace of the very humor it asperses, or be in certain quarters classified as "satire." So much today is called satire that was once content to be called spoofing; and so much *is* satire-of-a-kind today from no wish or ability to spoof. The answer lies partly in the topical or terminological nature of today's jokes, in the prevalence of headline humor (so that in Broadway shows the target is actually changed daily.) But the answer lies partly, too, in the *tone*, which almost gloatingly points up what is malignant in our lives, and has a sting that is hurtful and not healing. Now it is the essence of true humor for the humorist to ally himself with the joke; to be, as it were, a fellow-victim or culprit, a me-too in presumption or folly. The very victory—in largeness of spirit, in abdication of ego —lies in confessing defeat. But where humor is a form of honest admission, and shows a willingness to go naked, satire is a form of castigation, and has need to go armed. Humor is self-therapy, satire is doctor's medicine. But today's satire is too often a kind of illicit and perverted humor, which no more purges than it remonstrates. One does not display oneself as fellow-sufferer or fool, but as fellow-conspirator or knave. Where humor admits to being as human as the next man, today's satire shrugs at being as inhuman. It is more than cynical; it encourages cynicism. It serves neither society nor itself; it discharges bile and itself grows more bilious.

Obviously, the true satirist may fail of restoring health to society; may even, himself, remain sick. But, except as society perversely mocks or misreads him, he cannot *aggravate* its ills. And the passionate satirist may, of course, grow sick or mad from anger or despair. Swift, while straining to make "vice and folly bleed," spattered himself with rage and loathing. But Swift did make vice and folly bleed. Swift did bring great pressure on Britain; and to Ireland, great relief. Swift did, as few others, bring down satire's knout on society's skin. But he, as few others, could also, with the feather of playfulness, tickle humanity's hide. And as almost no other, he could make of the feather a lash. Every child has been playful with him, and, when grown up, felt in the same story condemnation and protest. And Swift is merely an easy starting-point for a canvass of playfulness as character-

istic of great natures, and great cultures. Without playfulness, seriousness itself is orphaned, and brought up
by a pompous guardian to become a solemn bore. And if
some one so scarred and riven as Swift, or so thin-
skinned and venomous as Pope, can become through
playfulness charmingly human, how much more must a
Dr. Johnson or a Jane Austen or a Dickens? But of these
we expect it, from their abounding wit or high spirits.
Moreover—which accounts for my restricted geography—playfulness has been very specially an English
or Irish gift, as palpable in Keats as in Byron, in Horace
Walpole as in Sydney Smith, in Sterne as in Oscar Wilde,
in Goldsmith as in Max Beerbohm. It has bubbled up in
a host of public men—Sir Thomas More, Wilkes, Sheri-
dan, Canning; and of reclusive ones—Gray, Cowper,
Fitzgerald, Lewis Carroll, Housman. I confess that it carries with it no certificate of moral excellence—it has
perished at times on the gallows; nor proof of financial
solvency—it has languished very often in the gutter. But
in every social sphere, and at all intellectual levels—in
sickroom and ballroom, in trenches and near thrones—
it has brought great, and much-needed, pleasure. If no
bastion of civilization, it is at least a breathing space.
Yet, despite how many new devices we have for laughter today, and how many new subjects, playfulness—at
least in its true honest classic form—seems in great
decline.

What has caused this decline is not easily formulated; but we might, to begin with, ask what playfulness
requires to flourish. "The play impulse" is certainly a

very pillar of Freud, and all its diverse manifestations
have produced a mountain of reading-matter. But whole
libraries involving the spirit of play have not kept playfulness briskly circulating, nor can we expect those who
guard to beget it. For the playfulness that was now the
salt, and now the leaven, of civilized commerce; that for
anxiety has been a cocktail and for melancholy an opi-
ate, has in terms of fancy the same dartingness of mind
that—in terms of imagination—nourishes seriousness.
The English have been the most playful of nations from
being the most poetic—or, more precisely, at once the
most poetic and most infantilist. Their nostalgia for the
nursery is so intense that a part of them has always re-
mained there. Yet their genius for nonsense has also
achieved a constant opulent adult bloom; the nonsense
behind their playfulness has flowered as sense and sur-
realism alike. And one of the great virtues of playfulness,
tossing its colored balls so high in the air, is that they
often plunge down and explode, a-glitter with malice, yet
breaking no bones and smashing no friendships. For the
high civilized virtue of playfulness is that, unlike most
forms of ragging and all forms of satire, it is reciprocal
in spirit, communal in design. In its social form every
one, upon some fanciful premise or absurd pretense,
improvises, elaborates, reorders. The tit-for-tats are made
into building blocks; the wild allegations become plot
devices; the deranged ascriptions act as open sesames.
The procedure is much the same, whether played by
two tots or a dozen savants: something creatively im-
provised, now airy, now headlong, now mad. Yet in its

effect it can be critical—devilishly so. But here the awareness of distance, the atmosphere of unreality, the safeguard of disguise, provide something no less bullet-proof than lethal. In playfulness there can indeed be method in the madness, and serious words spoken in jest, and prodigious sayings out of the mouth of babes. At the same time, a really proper playfulness must not wholly deviate into sense, nor add real injury to insult, nor remove the button from the foils, nor put weights inside the boxing gloves. The rules of the game are summed up in the title of it. Whenever it becomes more spiteful than playful; or more personal, or more pedantic, or more realistic; or whenever it becomes obsessive, its playfulness has curdled. The game has to do in the end with marksmanship rather than targets, for technically one may only fire blanks.

I would prefer to think of the preceding paragraph as an "analysis" of playfulness rather than as something honoring its memory. Perhaps it isn't falling into decline but is simply changing color, adopting new styles and different costumes. I may be looking for it in sweater and skirt, or even bonnet and shawl, when it has taken to slacks, or bikinis. But choosing my models from literature and life, from Falstaff and Hal impersonating Hal and the King, or from Johnson and Boswell impersonating Falstaff and Hal, or from things in Keats's letters, or Walpole's, or Lamb's; or from the muffin scene in *The Importance of Being Earnest,* or this scene or that in *Alice in Wonderland,* I find little, among people under forty, with the same fizz and gaiety to their fancifulness.

I find little that is both childlike and civilized, so that one might say "Let's play history" in the spirit of "Let's play house." Even pretendedly innocent merriment fails in an age whose one object is *touché,* and not necessarily with buttoned foils. Now, playfulness must not *begin* as a ploy for malice; it may, at most, lightly and wildly beget it. The architecture of today's jesting is, like architecture generally, functional; the architecture of playfulness is extravagant and rococo. The Brighton Pavilion, to turn to actual architecture, is a masterpiece of playfulness, just as it gave rise to a perfect piece of playful wit: Sydney Smith said that it looked "as though St. Paul's Cathedral had come down and littered."

The fact that, for painful reasons, people so often shun reality today and live inside fantasy worlds, has perhaps killed any wish to let playfulness build them. We make jokes today of our dissatisfactions; we jest at scars from having felt the wound. But since we are aware that our jokes exist to massage our resentments, and since the truly playful people I know are no nobler or "better adjusted" than others, their secret must lie in contriving a true holiday escapism, in allowing even malice a Mardi Gras domino. When I enumerated, a moment ago, the traits that must not outweigh playfulness, I was merely trying to define it. But it now occurs to me that it is precisely those traits that are working to destroy it. Our public entertainers are, too many of them, needling personalities rather than *personae.* From the harmless Hope-Crosby running gags to the TV headliners who load their fun with feuding, or the sick-humor boys who base their fun on fear, or those who make targets of themselves, calming their neuroses by commercializing them—much in all this joking that doesn't seem too spiteful, seems too personal or realistic or obsessive. Often "playfulness" seems a mere dodge: we are meeting egotism and exhibitionism undisguised; the fanciful inventions have all-too-factual echoes; the satire isn't even born of the headlines but is brewed from the gossip columns. The point, these days, is how near every wisecrack hits home, *and* how messed-up is the home life. It would seem that when the genteel was routed, it revengefully took the genial with it. To find today the wacky geniality of the Joe Cooks and Ed Wynns and Robert Benchleys, we must import it in a slightly foreign form, in a Flanders and Swann, in a *La Plume de Ma Tante.*

In any case, there can be no Mardi-Gras escapism when make-believe traces back to the abrasively real, and geniality, airiness, fizz are not possible. Some current comedy, to be sure, isn't meant to be playful; is meant, quite properly, to have bite. But much that professes to be "all in fun" not just hits too close to home but comes even closer to harshness. Even in our depicting how uncivilized we are, there is less of the satirist's eye than the dyer's hand. And with, as it were, such a public image of humor, what will it be in private? One can pretty well imagine four or five bright young TV or publicity executives, jovial after a few drinks, joined to the same business address, turning playful. One can imagine them saying "Let's play Office," and reshuffling the staff, with this one in the doghouse, that one on the hot seat, a third one kicked upstairs. One more drink, and present company might be included. "I'd know it was you, old boy, the minute the phone rang."—"No, you wouldn't, because I wouldn't phone—I'd just send you a memo."

When we get round to most intellectuals today, playfulness, rather than showing a jagged edge, lacks even a proper blade. It is with today's typical intellectuals that the dearth of playfulness is most pronounced. Most of them don't even approve of playfulness in theory. This is partly from their being ponderous, but partly too from *its* having no point to it: for intellectuals, everything must have a point, or provide a target. Otherwise, how can it be fitted into a larger "framework"; otherwise—and worse—how can it be *taught*? Only if playfulness, whose great point is its lack of significance, can somehow be endowed with it, will it achieve approval. Endow it with enough, and it can have a *Stammbaum, a rationale,* a *mystique,* and doubtless a college career (English 127 f: *Playfulness Since 1931.* Limited to 20.)

Even where intellectuals' playfulness isn't too academic, it has still something earthbound about it, too specific a frame of reference. Half the fun of the playful is what proves brusquely unforeseeable about it, or inadvertently apt. In its flight from reality, it must most of all flee the obvious; its best yardstick is a broomstick; its great weapon a tripped-over land mine. But with intellectuals today, even their lunacies must have a local habitation and a name. There are, of course, other and sounder reasons for their unplayfulness. A big one is the state of the world, creating tensions for which this form of escape proves inadequate; better forms seem to be drink, gambling, fast cars. And perhaps an age that has outdone the wildest fiction with its missiles and its orbiting finds playful fancy by no means fanciful enough.

Still, too many people often fail of playfulness today because of an insistent self-importance. This isn't merely ego or self-regard; many very playful people are passionately self-regarding. With intellectuals it may almost stem from a too unconfident self-regard, from having to *assert* an importance they cannot take for granted. Clearly today's intellectuals can't accept an element in playfulness that quite goes beyond the trivial or pointless; an element of sheer silliness, of casting out all intellectual values. For, as high spirits mount, those values must vanish. The moment arrives when a bad pun is better than a good one; when a non-sequitur is the only true logic; when a wrong date or a garbled quotation is the only true learning; and a roll in the mud the best proof of a ride in the clouds. Amid all this, what alone must persist is a civilized awareness of how silly it is— the sense that one can be utterly beneath criticism from being altogether beyond status. The slightest fear that you may be suspected of knowing no better is fatal; and with many intellectuals, just that is the worst fear there is. What they seldom grasp, too, is that one's playful self should be one's more generous self. One's irritations should stroll off arm-in-arm with one's inhibitions, and the whole effect of the make-believe suggest a fairy wand and not a painful weapon. It is exactly this that can prove so restorative, so therapeutic; but perhaps I, too, begin to endow playfulness with a *Stammbaum*, a *rationale*, a moral framework. And perhaps, what is more, I should.

· 6 ·

In late middle age, something beyond our Walter-Mitty self soberly starts wondering about our epitaph. If we are writers, we hope of course to be read and esteemed, and survive at least in references and footnotes. But actually our epitaphs—so brief, so one-sided—aren't much to the purpose; what we would really like to see is our obits: less the morning-after-death newspaper account than the judicious column-and-a-half we hope for in a sound journal of opinion. As we envision it, it will be forbearing but not sanctimonious; and, rather by its tone than by any specific statement, will convey what we were and what perhaps we shall be. We want to know how we really struck our contemporaries. For they, despite all the talk about the perspective of posterity, would alone have understood us on our own terms; they alone had shared our tensions and guessed at our temptations, and had the aptest sense for reading between the lines.

In any case, my vanity, in the matter of posterity, is pretty manageable. On shorter terms it has the usual reckless cravings, against which I hope my years can raise a moderately restraining hand. At least in any autobiographical passages it will content itself with middle-aged commentary; will sanction no scenes of childhood, or indiscretions of youth; no letters from kind ladies or great men. I shall, in other words, be brief. ("I was short," said a clergyman, speaking of his sermon to Canning, "to avoid being tedious." Said Canning: "But you *were* tedious.")

Yet in writing about oneself, the most dangerous pit-fall is in being, not tedious, not egotistical, but coy. So long as we are self-conscious, which means self-regardful, we can hardly not be coy at times. Coyness is a rather comically pathetic fault, a miscalculation in which, by trying to veil the ego, we let it appear stark naked; in which—and this is the nub—while hoping to gain approval, we give offense. Yet coyness, however impure in motive, does have an awareness about it that goes beyond mere awareness of self. It does have a kinship with all the fictitious politeness that contrives to make life run smoother. Why should the one kind of disclaimer seem courteous, and the coy kind objectionable? I suppose it means that to be palpably insincere about others is one thing, and about ourselves quite something else. In social conversation, coyness can be irritating enough. For we are being asked to make up the difference between the speaker's real idea of his value and his coyly reduced price; and the demand puts us as much out of humor as out of pocket. But coyness in print—a writer's coyness—is ultimately far more objectionable; partly for permitting no return in kind; but chiefly for seeming not just a human fault, but an artistic one. The *writer* should know better; or how to manage better. When T. S. Eliot writes: "In a poem of mine called *The Waste Land*,"

it is—for the kind of audience Eliot is addressing—as
though the President should say, "In a residence of mine
called The White House." When Max Beerbohm speaks
of the very work of his we are reading as "this wretched
book," we feel a double annoyance—first because of his
impudence (if that's what he thinks of it) in foisting
it on us; but again because he is getting too much ironic
satisfaction from what he is saying. For an ironic remark that excludes rather than delicately solicits the
reader must always irritate. It is oftenest, indeed, the
ironic temperament that is given to coyness. What is
self-depreciatory gratifies the writer *at the moment of
writing,* both as a private joke, and for how devil-may-
care he thinks he is being about his public image.

A writer's coyness is a very ticklish business because
it is so tactical a one. The problem of self-portraiture
can be openly, candidly treated; it is some kind of effort at
truth. The problem of self-presentation, being far more
oblique, being involved with "approach," compels vanity
to be sinuous and even sly. It tends to destroy, not only
any effort at truth, but all instinct of naturalness. And
just here, from possessing sensibility, the coy writer falls
down oftener and fares worse than the not over-sensitive
one. The writer who talks straight out about himself or
his work seldom offends; the coy writer is only topped, I
would think, by the extremely conceited writer. Frequent
coyness, the one real fault in a Beerbohm, is about as
displeasing, as, say, the self-congratulatory, Goethe-
identifying first-person writing of a Thomas Mann. And
the contrast between the two men is between a too ele-

gantly obsequious French waiter, and the smug pompous German he is waiting on.

· 7 ·

As against telling the story of one's life, one's attempting a short harvest of reactions about life in general may be far less judicious than it seems. In a sense, greater danger lurks in a chapter of personal observations than in a whole volume of memoirs. The memory, to be sure, can be more tedious than the mind, and more untrustworthy; but factually, pictorially, it will often be unique. Every man's life, honestly recaptured and properly told, has a certain interest; how many men's reflections have? Moreover, ransacking our memories, we can turn young and amusing and intrepid; with our minds we grow sententious and elderly. And, in attempting to sum life up, we have to fear not just the youthful valedictorian's indulgence in platitude, but the oldster's habituation to cant. It is in trying to flee from cant, indeed, that one often falls into coyness. For, instead of just getting up at sixty to speak our piece, what we do is get up to introduce and explain ourselves as the speaker: the gentleman who will address you this evening insists he's very inexperienced at this kind of thing . . . hopes you'll be good enough to make allowances . . . didn't know English till he was fourteen. . . . wishes he could be listening to *you* . . .

And what plagues any late-middle-aged valedictory is how true its platitudes are; and how consoling. One grapples with the latest "thinker," and, granting him certain private insights or new twists, what seems rewarding seems generally reminiscent. But if the clichés at first console, they soon disquiet us; they are so ignobly relentless, so shoddily right. In all the homely adages that fifty years have proved sound, in all the worldly aphorisms that forty years have proved valid, there is not much generosity, not much benevolence. The counsels, it turns out, that we can most safely trust are those that warn against trustfulness. And if we shift, from a certain shame, to the truism pervaded with altruism, it smacks of comforting humbug. Yet, if doubtfully good advice, more humane and large-minded counsels still qualify as sound risks. One repudiates any thought that love conquers all, or that poverty ennobles, or that life is beautiful. Yet one has come to know how much love can sustain, or life can enrich, and even how suffering fortifies. And by late middle age, opposites have joined hands—the comic and the tragic, the pretended and the true. Suddenly, mythological shapes seem actual and living—man as centaur, half courage and half cowardice; man as werewolf, half kindly and half cruel. What is more, though almost every one's experience of life can be compressed into platitudes, scarcely any two people's platitudes would be exactly the same. In how one generalizes at sixty, one may come closest to seeming individual.

At sixty, at least some clichés have withered away: taking-the-long-view, for example. It is not just that for any one at sixty the long view seems more of a taunt than an injunction. It is that, having taken the long view of the long view, one is not too much impressed. At twenty, one could in principle decide for it—no need to get out of breath running toward every inviting prospect, or away from every threatening cloud; and at thirty, much that you had thought you wanted, you found you could nicely do without. But, all in all, the long view was decidedly more honored in the breach; and—when it was applied—proved too often to be just a euphemism, an evasion, a self-deception. It looked very pretty in the distance; closer up, the long view looked more like shirked duty, or sour grapes, or "It'll all come out in the wash."

It may be that any conflagration now affrighting us will seem a mere match flare three centuries hence. But *we* shall be less than the burnt match. And is seeing, say, Nazi Germany as a match flare a proof of perspective? For most of us, the long view is far oftener consoling than bracing. And to be of value, it must belong to us by temperament; it can't be forced on us by thought. Fine as a cosmic ideal, as just that it fails us in more human affairs. To take the long view of desegregation, for example, makes sense in view of the immense difficulties involved; but not where the difficulties are the slightest pretext for indecision or delay. To take the long view about TV—well, to *have* to take it after all these years suggests how crushingly far it has to go. To take the long view of ourselves is worst of all. To see ourselves as a kind of growth stock, making modest annual gains in reason and virtue, is rank wildcat speculation.

Sufficient to close a point or two higher on any particular day.

The long view seems as much cant as cliché. On the other hand, the idea that one can take no long view at all of today's nuclear world seems like cant-in-reverse—seems an excuse for being self-seeking, irresponsible, dead to values. It leads many people, however real their terrors of a nuclear world, into not a sane attitude of business-as-usual, but into a greedy one of business-as-never-before. It is as though the life-and-death competitiveness between ourselves and the Soviet Union has become the model for a personally frenzied material struggle; as though a fierce status war between two nations has infected every Jones and Smith in Westport.

The high virtue of short views is, of course, that one *has* to decide, is driven to act; and very often with a sharp sense of loss and gain. But at sixty, the short view too has its dangerous side. One has, at sixty, few hopes of changing the world; so that any really long view has vanished, perhaps to leave behind a sort of highly opinionated petrifaction. At sixty, along with "enlightened" outlooks, there goes weakened eyesight. Or is even eyesight the trouble?—how keenly do we always try to look at things? How often, in looking around, is one not really looking back? How often does "I've seen it all before" save us from even taking a look? A little dutifully, one reads certain new writers. But after fifty, one's tastes and attitudes (and the basis for them) are in most of us formed; one's new enthusiasms are likely to be for what was there all the time and one had earlier passed by.

On the other hand, what might be called the journalism of life still attracts one. The front page of life does so, of course, from self-interest or citizenry; the crime news and sporting news have an appeal; as have sex, and amusement, and life's comic sections. Indeed, one develops a real interest in picturesque trivia, and remembers the skeets champion of New Zealand while forgetting the Premier, and all the wife-killers in Finland but not one of the poets. But it is precisely as journalism —journalism in the old ephemeral sense, before it was riddled with commentators—that one responds to it.

Of course one hasn't petrified; but the very exaggeration serves as a euphemism. *Set* or *prejudiced* would prove too damning, might fit one too well. But, whatever the word used, it gives the thought of wisdom at sixty a decided jolt. For such wisdom is predicated of having lived long enough to compare procedures and philosophies, to note causes and effects, to grasp how well systems worked and reputations wore, and which were new beacons and which merely new brooms. One had seen credos discredited and causes betrayed; the tree planted and the tree bearing fruit. The chief trouble with the comparative method is how often the new tends to lose out to the old.* And this seems truest where the mind is most critical. For the mind must always be judging; and, as it grows older, this can mean prejudging and misjudging, or that the more extensive the background, the

---

* This of course doesn't apply to new devices and contrivances for making life easier; or to advances in fields— medicine, science, whatever the case may be—where one is ignorant or ill-versed.

((157))

more is the foreground on trial. To take a homely example from married life: every wife is confronted in the
kitchen with the ghost of husband's mother—*her* apple
pie; *her* . . . gee, she called it stew too, but this isn't it.
A like spectre hovers over most of one's sixty-year-old
judgments—young Mr. X's handling of dialogue; or
theory of history; or response to baroque.

Happily—and in a sense, rightly—one feels no shame
for one's set reactions. Every period of life has its particular desideratum. For youth it is independence; for
early manhood, advancement; for early middle age,
position; for late middle age, full expression of temperament. Such an expression is perhaps the least wrongful
form of selfishness, for one much less indulges one's will
or appetites than one's attitudes and whims. And if a
cultivated man near sixty isn't given to crotchets, he will
be very poor company for himself. I would place very
high the *moral* value of crotchets; they can be a non-
malignant form of what might have been forms of oppression and despotism. To be sure, they can bore other
people past belief—having to hear father explain the
only right way to brush one's teeth, or an infallible way to
cure hiccups. And his family may blush at his rotting
old bathrobe, or grow pale at his idea of a good place to
go for dinner.

His relations with the young are, very often, in different case. Every man his age who hasn't petrified, or
isn't far gone in priggishness, wants the approval of the
young members of his own profession; on how they react
to him, indeed, rests the proof of how far he has sur-

vived. Their approval—of the artist, the intellectual, the professional man—is two-pronged: of what he himself is like, and of what he has achieved. Having his work approved touches the more acute desire; but that he should be approved of by the young is desired for a half-comic reason—the fact that of all people the gifted, inquiring young are the most intolerant. Winning their favor may not be the highest homage, but it is almost the greatest feat. They have a saturation point for most oldsters in their field: so long as he can be revealing about matters they care about, or can be brightly reminiscent, or can talk shop somewhat on their terms, he offers welcome information or enlightenment. It takes a good deal more to be welcomed for himself; and not till the young consent to argue with him, and disagree with him, and get zestfully excited with him, is it his self that is being shown respect, and not his age. The great celebrity may win ceremonious homage; for any one less, the accolade is not "You may be right, sir!" but a nice, firm, egalitarian "You're nuts."

In any fruitful commerce between generations, there must be a lack of priggishness on both sides. In wanting, at sixty, to be chosen, one should be choosy as well. My crochets go beyond bananas and bathrobes, they can involve hackles and profanity. My concern for the young is for the *young*. They have to win my approval for me to care very much for theirs. They won't necessarily forfeit it if they spit in my eye; they will, if they look down their noses. They won't necessarily forfeit it if they speak slightingly of Shakespeare; they will if some fashionable pundit plainly taught them to. They won't forfeit it if they've never seen a single Magnasco canvas; they may, if against that, they have read *The Spoils of Poynton* six times. They must be authentically *young;* by preference brilliant, charming, deferential, sympathetic; but quite allowably hotheaded, opinionated, intolerant. They can be shocking; can even set out to be shocking; but they must not, in any prim or icily pedantic way, be shocked. Nor, having bellowed in one corner of the room, may they bootlick in another. If I take a didactic tone about them, it is from having at bottom a romantic regard.

Assuming a *rapport* between intellectual and artistic generations, there at once arises the matter of influence, of discipleship. Clearly every older man wants esteem and some ability to be impressive; and discipleship-at-a-distance, when the Master's work and not he is reverenced, can have great value. It can have it, again, when the discipleship is creative—the apprentice value of the Renaissance workshop, or in a Maupassant's relation to a Flaubert, or perhaps when the *cher maître* is a reigning convention, as much a part of being twenty-one as the *petite amie.* But every sensitive and perceptive older man should as much deprecate for himself as discourage in the young, being elevated as a Master. Among the homelier reasons, he will not feel bruised when he finds he is no longer. Having disciples is in the end like having children, only not with love but with self-love preeminent. Disciples will not just grow away from you; you must in all conscience encourage them to. Worse, you must be prepared for them to tire of you, see through you, turn against you. The Master who will not assume such risks is potentially not deliverer but despot. Today, moreover, when spheres and schools of influence, at any rate in a public and vocal sense, are much oftener critical than creative, of the classroom rather than the atelier, the relation of master and pupil seems especially dangerous.

All in all, I think the only truly good relationship between the generations must be one of reciprocal advantage, which is to say of fundamental equality. Here, again, there is an analogy with one's children—the idea that you are entitled to respect and deference on pain that you seldom exact it. Here too there is the fact that you know much more at the start, but with every passing day know a little less; and that, whether or not you have as much to learn as to teach, you may certainly have as much to hear about as to tell. Decidedly, the young want to be taught, and doubtless desire a father image. But even then the Master must take his *role* far more seriously than he takes himself; should indeed find it a pleasurable duty to proclaim his own fallibility before the fact leaks out. As for the young, those of them are much the best off who instinctively worship not masters but masterpieces; who turn sedulous apes without turning sheep. They are the best off, too, if amid great artistic loves and exalted fervors, they dally a little with the demi-monde, and are "had" at times by spellbinders. Second-rate admirations have one notable virtue—while often helping to emancipate us, they rather quickly emancipate us from themselves. I have said somewhere of Mencken, and his value to the young in the 1920s, that he was not the big city, but only the train that took you there. And this was to define rather than damn him. Indeed, its forms of transport can serve culture almost as well as its actual terminals; and the *idea* of transport—of movement and sightseeing and change of scene—is absolutely essential. There are terminal things in culture and in our own lives; but they can all too easily acquire a big-city parochialism or a walled-city isolation. No Master can ever be a terminus, at least without in some sense becoming a tomb.

·IV·

The Writer at Large

For some two thousand years the world has been told of the irascibility of poets; and has scarcely needed to be told. The more intimate and anecdotal side of history abounds in artists' rages and revenges—against their patrons, their families, their fellows. From envy or malice or frustration or guilt they have hurled epithets, and more than epithets; have broken bones and flashed knives and fired off pistols; and burned their own hands off and cut off their own ears. The artist, in an almost sensational form, is a man of passion. If, from his work, he often appears reflective and sedentary, the public yet visualizes him in postures of illicit lovemaking or supine drunkenness or foul-mouthed defiance. The public *wants* to think of him as scandalous, dangerous, glamorous: Villon and Cellini, Rochester and Casanova, Burns and Byron; Swinburne and Rimbaud; T. E. Lawrence and Dylan Thomas—the procession is extensive.

The public is largely right in asking the artist to embody much of what he envisions—to have displayed the grander, or at any rate, the more fiery qualities of unrighteous living. Or, if he was not to be luridly demonic, he should seem picturesquely doomed; if not muscular like Jack London, then tuberculous like Keats; if not in the saddle like Scott, then on a sofa like Mrs. Browning, or in a sealed room like Proust. And if not dying for a cause, he should die for a crime, or a woman. Though the public upbraids and even persecutes the artist for not being domesticated and law-abiding, at heart it deprecates the thought that he isn't.

To be sure, the various flamboyant guises in which the public envisions him are not those in which he is generally found. All too often he has been a don or a professor or a clergyman—Sterne, Gray, Emerson, Arnold, Santayana, Newman, Housman, Kingsley, Pater, Herrick, Herbert, Donne and how many more; or he has worked in an office like Lamb, or at the custom-house like Hawthorne, or as an insurance executive like Wallace Stevens. And rather than tragically consumptive like Keats, he has been dyspeptic like Carlyle, or just monstrously overweight like Chesterton. The lack of dash and brilliance in artists is not unusual, if only because they save such qualities for their art; it is commonly the second-rater who thumps the personality pedals. When the young Coventry Patmore pays his first call on Leigh Hunt, and Hunt, after keeping him waiting two hours, enters impressively and booms out: "This is a beautiful world, Mr. Patmore," we feel it has been carefully planned. But would we, sitting next to them in the public coach, have spotted Mozart or Keats or Jane Austen?

Yet, though we know that writers can be drab and clerical as well as gin-soaked and steeped with vice, we seldom wonder whether in times past they had the small, suburban faults that can make our contemporary familiars so rasping and dislikable. We know that Dr. Johnson could be an outrageous bully and Pope a venomous wasp; that Hazlitt was sometimes truculent and Landor often intemperate; that Wilde posed, and Wordsworth prated. Lamb has recorded how he and his friends played a game about famous people in history they would have liked to meet. We, in the same spirit, might speculate on writers we would have wanted as house guests—or not wanted. One thinks of Tolstoy; not least of the tradition that all day long they had to be beating up omelets for him in the kitchen, so that at the exact moment he demanded one it would be ready, and just right. One imagines Henry James in one's living room—just when one wanted to slump in one's chair and in one's thinking and one's word choice: the old Henry James might well have been a more terrifying house guest than the young Rimbaud. Chekhov would perhaps have been the nicest guest and the least troublesome; but then, he would have been perhaps the most observant.

The house-guest game comes off, I think, as rather more than a game; it makes us consider—as matters involving the dead seldom do—those particular small irritations that much less characterize a writer than demote him to every-day stature: his annoying little mannerisms; his way of being *in* the way; or demanding; or peevish. The public, all in all, is right in its conception—largely a misconception—of the artist as often irresponsible and "immoral" but also grandly scornful of the restraints the public itself submits to; as given to dissent and defiance; as possessing a generosity of emotion that can get him in trouble, and one about money that can leave him in rags. The public, given to imagining a great writer as its house guest, would doubtless assume he would walk naked into the living room; probably seduce the daughter of the house and certainly the maid; let the bath tub run over, receive collect long-distance calls at 3 a.m., drink one's whiskey openly at breakfast and smuggle more of it into his room; leave the room a shambles on departing, and borrow money to get to his next destination.

Well, perhaps. In any case, the artist—aroused by a sense of life's blind injustices and of humanity's hard-eyed ones—has often been notably, nobly generous; been steadily courageous; been again and again the pulse, the voice, the conscience of his time. In addition, he has spoken up for art, and sacrificed and gone without for it; and it is not to be supposed that in rising above intimidation, in railing against venality and hypocrisy and oppression, he has not been glaringly human too, and sometimes inhuman. No sensible person does suppose that. Plainly the artist can be a brute to live around, and fall frighteningly short as husband or father or citizen. As, in terms of conscience, he says *Ich kann nicht anders,* so of his character he may cry *Sono che sono.* Hence it is no shock to find in him much that the respectable find shocking; to encounter swollen egos, voracious appetites, wayward tastes; powerful, even ungovernable, emotions; irritable, even vituperative, moods. These seem the price, or the penalties, of the creative gift; the dark side, as it were, of the moon. Crotchets, too, it is no surprise to find in writers: call them neuroses and it would be unthinkable not to find them. Even senseless blind spots and shameful prejudices may appear. Usually, when we encounter these last, we perceive miserliness as born of insecurity; or distrust, of early betrayal. If we allow that the artist is some one who feels intensely, we must also concede that he can feel intensely and wrong. All this is of long standing, and is no more to plead for the artist than indict him.

Still, there are times—there are traits—that seem specially forgivable, and others that give one pause. The artist's assumed superiority, like any one else's, predicates a responsibility. His being privileged (as most enlightened people would allow he is) to go unhindered by ordinary conventions and restraints argues that freedom shall not just be self-indulgent. About him there must be some form of *noblesse oblige*. It is a very particular form, it has nothing to do with the codes of conduct that seem married to the phrase. But it does imply that, as he is specially esteemed for qualities of understanding, sensibility, large-mindedness, these things he must not betray. It does insist, that despite a hundred things he may succumb to, to a few things—in his writings, at least— he may not descend.

Obviously we are not to condemn the writer by the man. The man may be stained with iniquity and hideous from vice; may have lied, stolen, raped, murdered. His poems or novels, whether they document his life or disguise it, are only to be judged by artistic standards, on a basis of his talent and sense of truth. This we take for granted. But there are times, it seems to me, when we are entitled to assess the man by way of the writer. Allowing for the huge disparity between his values as an artist and his virtues as a man, surely there can be certain denials, certain betrayals, of the one by the other that call for judgment. Some of the "denials" are comic enough to be forgiven, or classic enough to be foreseen. We all protest the sufferings of the working class and bellow at the scrubwoman. We all of us bewail the tragic burden of humanity and fume over a button off our coat.

This is not quite it. The writer, in a pinch, may be forgiven almost anything done on impulse; or from temper; or "without premeditation." But when there has been time to think, the man *can* be set against the writer. And, short of being psychopathic, he can be found guilty for displaying qualities he is known to denounce; for proving, in cold print, mean or petty, rancorous or self-righteous, grudge-bearing or uncharitable. He is hardly less guilty when, in print, he is brash and pushing from self-interest, or sniping or small-minded from envy.

Writers, to be sure, suffer from such weaknesses in the—often inordinate—degree that they suffer from vanity. A writer's vanity is inflamed by his arrogance about his gifts, and even more by his anxiety about them.

((170))

It is further inflamed by his particular acute sensibility: with no effort at all, you can step on his toes or get under his skin. In this careerist age, where so much is brutally aggressive, his vanity is both more enlarged and more exposed. In an age so publicity-ridden, the writer, again, has the spotlight no less than the limelight to worry about; the publicity he would shun as well as the publicity he would seek. His own voice carries today as never before; and, as never before, the voice of others becomes audible to him. Most writers that one respects do have, as men, the decency to resist, in print or in public, their shabbier impulses and meaner thoughts; and, when they *would* quarrel, to be forthright about it; and, when they would trade insults, to be urbane. But how often, how increasingly often, today in that Greater Literary World that embraces journalistic and academic suburbs, does one encounter a small-mindedness far worse than spontaneous malice; a self-interest failing only from brashness to be sly. And how often does one encounter it in print—and next, understandably in rebuttal. Compared with other artists, writers have of course, besides greater articulateness, the constant *power* of print. The malice of composers or painters perishes when merely waspish, and only survives when dowered with wit. But writers can do infinitely more than reshape their lunch-table flings for the printed page. They can exploit every verbal outlet, from a letter to the editor to a *roman à clef;* all forms of literary mention, including the lack of any.

As symptoms of this, consider how many novels keep appearing today with academic settings, that are plainly and punishingly key novels as well. And for the most part, how parochial and satirically barren they are. But if their narrow vision is deplorable, what is genuinely sad is the narrowed experience that ordains it: this campus world is the only one they know. But sadder still, what pettiness goes into the exposure of pettiness! As for writers who carry every unfavorable criticism leveled against them as a grievance to the grave, what juts up about so many of them is their own need—and knack— for being acid, their own love of the poisoned dart.

Today's whole literary atmosphere of malice direct and malice retaliatory is the more pronounced, of course, for the huge gossip-column element, the calculated name-calling, in contemporary life. Here writers, far from combatting a form of pernicious journalism, have often taken to copying it. They are also, in a sense, by virtue of their prestige, making it seem more reputable. So much that is snipingly personal gets into print on one pretext or another, that we might set opposite the old gag that if you pilfer from enough people it's not plagiarism but research, a newer one that if you repeat enough people's tattle it's not gossip but documentation. To be sure, much written about life and society today involves personal references and "revealing" anecdotes. But much, too, has far less documentary than pure gossip value; and has behind it, even as gossip, less a wish to amuse than a need to be spiteful. One very minor sidelight possibly deserves mention. Today's emphasis on documentation, which so often leads to monumental dullness, has—right in academic circles— encouraged a form of it that shall at all costs not be dull. More and more often, one gets asked by thesis-writing graduate students to supply quite personal information on their chosen subjects. Some of this could well have value; but, along with much that seems irrelevant to an academic critical study, much seems inquired after for what suggests a kind of chatty *New Yorker* profile or *Time* cover story.

The academic writer has, from far back, had hard sledding, with work that, condemned to slow progress, culminates in bad pay. Today, as I have said elsewhere, he is coming more into his own, notably off campus. But, while an attitude has understandably developed to try to enjoy the best of both worlds, a type has emerged exhibiting the worst of both. The new type, in his campus role, can be petty, pedagogical, increasingly authoritarian; while off-campus he is no less power-seeking, but pushy in method and brash in approach. He leaves no stone unturned; and if not yet up to playing the quick-change artist, he is all too ready to play it. What gave me, frankly, malicious pleasure when it got known that I was quitting as drama critic for *Time,* was the stirring and rustling of highbrow connoisseurs of art, of high-minded custodians of morality, who immediately phoned or wrote to me about getting the job. Earlier they had been given to deplore mass journalism, not to speak of the Luce publications. It was instructive to learn—without asking —the ennobling reasons that prompted their new attitude: a weariness of academic confines; a wish to endow benighted audiences with enlightened views;

a desire to make middle-browism the bride of high culture.

I can understand and applaud the wish of the immured man-of-letters to feel the stir of the outside world and to taste its fruits; can strongly approve it as the invigorating envy of some one with more than just dust in his nostrils and ink in his veins. But the new breed I am talking about—he is almost always under forty—often reveals, along with a peculiar academic coldness, something coldbloodedly careerist. He wants power, not just prestige; and in his tactics can be as ruthless as he may be obsequious in his tone. As he gains in importance, he gains in self-importance even more; and the pale academic image, the scant academic means that alone excused his pushiness are valid no longer. And when pettiness of spirit * is fanned by self-righteousness, or slinking malice strides forth in moral robes, surely the writer or intellectual falls lower than what he attacks. When we encounter what is at least very disquieting in men of ability and high rank—witness Mr. F. R. Leavis's attack on Sir Charles Snow—we see that, no matter what the assailant promulgated or cried down, something in *him* must be cried down. Mr. Leavis, with his acrimonious Evangelical mind, his authoritarian need for disciples, his, not just willingness to wound, but self-bestowed warrant to castigate, is a disturbing portent. Such a man—and it is only as a symbol that I speak of him—may indeed be a needed voice and a frequent mas-

* Strindberg was probably right in thinking pettiness the most ignoble of faults.

ter in the practice of *criticism*. But he sounds a rasping note, he sets an ungenerous example, in the progress of culture. For all his merit, such a man does not liberate, but enslaves. In the very bringing of truth, he inculcates intolerance.

In every age, no doubt, certain cultural forces have bred, in the artist, certain unworthy traits. I have said that in the face of what mean and petty forms his vanity can assume, a writer must react with a sense of *noblesse oblige*. But I don't know that *noblesse oblige* is precisely the nub. What seems true of many writers today— and a product of the times—is, rather than a lessened sense of obligation toward others, a lessened sense of respect for themselves. If there is anything a writer is aware of, it is his vanity. And if one's wounded vanity is forever trying to break through confining bars, to squirt acid or pelt rocks, surely one's pride should be standing guard as jailer. How fatuous we may all be from vanity, how we may preen ourselves or strike becoming poses; or cease to growl when properly courted, and purr when deftly stroked—that matters little; let us be as fatuous as we choose. Even how badly we act in the heat of the moment, when suddenly belted or stung, is pardonable enough. But that a week later, or a year later, we should—for no attack on our womenfolk's honor or mortal insult to our own—be meanly retaliatory in action, or indecently revengeful in print: against such things no writer can preach too often, particularly to himself. He must have too much pride to stoop so low, or even remember so long. He should months ago have composed the masterpiece of abuse and demolition he then tore up; or glorified his own nature with its talent for forgiveness; or foreseen for his enemy a hideous fate. At the worst, he should have been halted by a sense of analogy: shall he, this fine-grained serious man, this perspicacious novelist or torch-bearing professor, feud and backbite like any gossip columnist or publicity-mad cheapjack or TV star?

A writer's *literary* malice—his need to nail pretension and hypocrisy, to uncover hidden motives and pious disguises—is not just a legitimate part of his equipment, it is an extremely valuable one. It is his finest means for making a sort of protesting nudist colony of the human race. And to strip men naked, the writer need not go to the seventeenth century or to Outer Mongolia; he can stay close to home. He need not even write fiction or plays; he can review them, or write profiles; or biography; or autobiography. But, *artistically*, the crux here is not how malicious he is, but how genuinely a writer. The crux, humanly, is not how malicious but how free from self-interest. The crux, morally, is not how malicious but how free from pious self-deception. In the *true* artist, the rankling snub or festering slight will have sloughed off venom for wit, and coated anger with insight: the human need to strike back will have deferred to a professional concern for marksmanship. Nor is it always a matter of striking *back*. There are critics who gloatingly smite, for art's sake as they think. There are satirists who, in the craving to inflict pain on the victim, give small pleasure to the bystanders—and in time make targets of themselves. I don't insist that what I call malice in a writer's work can be transformed into something ennobling; enough if it is aerated by truly literary yeast, if it emerges as bread and not dough. And it must never pose as morality: one of its proper "malicious" aims is to shatter that pose in others.

I have overstressed all this: to many writers it does not apply in the least; in others there is much to redeem it. The true villain, in any case, is something that, like a small animal, has been nuzzling and nibbling away at our whole culture, and that by slowly altering our assumptions, has more and more altered our attitudes. In an age of rampant publicity, even those who normally shun publicity may feel the need of it at times to survive; or the value of it, to succeed; or the power of it, to demolish. The writer's own ego, in such an age, can so react to change as to prefer seeing his picture, let us say, to his face. In an age of syndicated scandal and wire-photo'd feuds, even reputable publications succumb to doubtful practices. Finally, a new false principle of Equal Time sanctions outrageous tactics, on the basis that it is all right to throw dirt so long as others have a chance to throw it back. Writers, moreover, are *encouraged* to get into hassles; and if they possess a real gift for tantrums, can carve out a splendid career.

Concurrently, in highbrow journalism, Mr. Prosz-Hahlo's controversial article will call forth a great mass of answers, some of them from the victims of it. Then, immediately following the letters, Mr. Prosz-Hahlo "replies." And he gets in all his original wacks, often harder, a second time; then flays half the readers who took issue with him. This, for all its air of editorial fairness, is quite unfair. Unless the letters to the editor have impugned Mr. Prosz-Hahlo's character, or demonstrably misrepresent vital facts or ideas, he has no right to answer. He must expect disagreement; and may not reappear to punish it.* But the Editor naturally wants a lively correspondence column, and to achieve it will often tolerate —indeed, cultivate—a climate of ill-natured arrogance and abuse. Owing to the age's love of personalities and gossip, today's writer is given every chance to be vocal and visible; owing to the age's no-holds-barred competitiveness, he too often resorts to very questionable tactics. Even many of the better writers who form part of our cultural Main Stream, are making of it an ever-muddier Mississippi. And this is all the worse in view of a kindred and surrounding contamination. For no longer is the *writer* alone professionally articulate and word-minded: by way of publicity, tabloid journalism, TV, words have become a vast irresponsible industry, and the power of words a tremendous—an often frighteningly jagged— weapon. Hence it is no longer enough that the writer use words with greater distinction than all the tradespeople of language. He must use them as a resounding offset to the tradespeople's; and not only toward far more enlightened ends, but in an immeasurably more generous spirit. After all, his protest against, let us say, the influence of TV on culture must lose force when he himself typifies the effect of TV on conduct.

* In the same way, letters to the editor that are needlessly abusive shouldn't be printed unless toned down by the sender. All too many people whose only published writing is their letter-writing bang away without adding insight to injury.

Conformity's Cultured

Sister

FROM CONFORMITY the intellectual world, in a kind of mass movement of its own, has happily preserved itself. Scarcely an intellectual one knows eats TV dinners or enters canasta tournaments. The higher-browed care as little for the fads of conventional society as for the fetishes of the business world; they have not been "integrated," they have not capitulated, they do not conform. At any rate, they do not conform to Conformity. But another danger still confronts them: over against the Scylla of conformity must be set the Charybdis of constriction. It is generally a weakness of the higher orders; in fact, a chief element in the constricted life is a repugnance to what surrounds the conformist one. And were constriction no more than this—no more than proof of independent values and finer tastes and sensibilities—it would plainly merit praise rather than scrutiny; it would come close to defining, today, the superior man. In a certain sense, indeed, the constricted man *is* the superior man. But at what cost he purchases his superiority, and in what mood he practises it, crucially lessens its value.

One must, of course, define what one means by constriction. We are so beset with clichés like "many-sidedness" and "outside interests" and with all the cant they engender, that I must say at once that a rich full life isn't what I'm talking about. It's not just that a variety of interests (bowling, pipe-collecting, cookout cuisine) can be mere Babbitry or (T'ang pottery, madrigal singing, and the French symbolists) can be mere dilettanteism; it's rather that constriction is not a matter of interests at all, but of attitude. We are beset again with clichés like "nonconformist," "individualist," "being out of step"; but this too is unessential. For it's not just that nonconformity can smack of pose; it's that constriction refers less to liberating oneself than to legislating for other people. We are, for a third thing, beset with clichés like "change of air," "seeing how the other half lives," and "getting out of a rut"; but ultimately this too is beside the point. For beyond what can be mere tourism or culture-nibbling in all this, constriction has far less to do with being a stay-at-home than with wearing blinkers.

A certain kind of "constricted life"—one with few interests but passionate ones—could easily, at a high level, be an ideal life. Society might look askance at it, society might suffer neglect from it—such a life can hardly foster much social-mindedness; but it might well create so complete a temperamental adjustment as to need no other kind. To *be* ideal, this sort of life must go, of course, with a certain sort of self, one that so serenely knows its own mind as to have no temptation to give other people a piece of it. Moreover, really knowing what it wants, it can stand firm, it can move fast, about what it doesn't want. One day in a famous town, one chapter of a famous book, one meeting with a famous man, may be all it needs to say No, and forever. But the rejection is at all times personal, not "intellectual"; and though it may constitute a gross error of judgment, it does not derive from an acquired prejudice or promulgate a received idea; it is empirical and one's own.

Today, again, there exists a form of constrictedness that is almost a form of protest, one that constitutes drawing in one's horns not against life but against a pernicious type of it. If often somewhat unwarranted, such constrictedness is hardly unreasonable: we all miss out on something good from steering clear of what isn't —miss out on delicious food because the restaurant looks dirty; fail to meet an interesting man because his brother is a bore. Frankly, there are times when this kind of guilt-by-association is what alone makes life workable; acquittal-by-examination could prove painfully time-consuming. We are thumbs down on much, say, in mass culture from a certain knowledge of much else in it, and the burned child is not morally obligated to risk being done to a crisp.

All the same, too much of this protest-constrictedness,

((181))

too fervent a membership in a movement against everything deemed "popular," "bourgeois," extroverted," *can*
be the point at which what is praiseworthy in the constricted life starts jostling what is dubious. Or is, at any
rate, the point where the cure becomes as dangerous as
the disease, the point where one wrong kind of culture
gives rise to another, where the rumpus room is exchanged for the vault. The constricted life, in its behavior, can here harm itself more than it helps its cause: for
one thing, because its aim is not reform but excommuni-
cation; for another, because purism is no real answer
to pollution. As I have already half-suggested, conformity today helps breed constriction—as, even a generation ago, it did not. Then the American protest against
bourgeois values took some form of bohemian or radical
living. The intellectual and artistic life evolved a world
of its own, but a world cheerfully experimental, unper-
turbedly nomadic, a world of freelances and expatriates,
of crazes and causes. Bored with middle-class standards,
people often flamboyantly scorned them, defied them,
attacked them; but always their real retort was to revel
in a life of their own. Moreover, the conformist symbols
—which they would have called middle-class or philistine or genteel—were *creatively* adduced and applied,
whether by novelists like Dos Passos and Sinclair Lewis,
or humorists like Ring Lardner, or hatchet-men like
Mencken. About the symbols and the satire there was
often, moreover, something rowdy—a sense of a joke,
an air of the zoo.

Oddly enough, as the butts of this satire grew less

crude, as they got "cultured" and cleaned up, the cultural situation got muddied; for *they* were now part of it. They, flocking to college, now acquired a veneer. Simultaneously, the young intellectuals, who twenty years earlier often never finished college, now more and more enrolled there for life. A culturally journalistic age gave way to a culturally academic one. And as the two groups, by both going to college, moved closer in background, elsewhere they moved farther apart. Once boisterously heckled, the philistine in his new guise was coldly glared at and cut dead. For those who cut him dead bore a new guise also. The old bohemian intellectual who had got into social and political movements, and sexual and personal messes, had too often given way to some one fussily, fastidiously literary, or laboriously, statistically sociological.

There was reason for this: the radical era that came after the bohemian one had mauled esthetic values and critical detachment; and these things now needed to be stressed. All too often, however, they were more than stressed; they were segregated. Art under fire gave way to art under glass. The academic world—often with a creative writer in residence, rather like fresh flowers in an unaired room—took to preserving culture not just by denouncing all the philistinism that had earlier led the attack, but by denouncing all the "journalism" that had earlier led the attacking. Suddenly the middlebrow became the great target; middle-class interests, the life *behind* middlebrowism, were a decidedly lesser concern. Indeed, the life behind literature came to be scamped or dismissed; only the life beneath it, only the patriarchal, the mythic, the symbolic, greatly mattered. Against the shards and thighbones of Homeric society, the conditions of a society that had produced one's own family were trivial.

At the outset, the double-barreled attack on bourgeois values and journalistic culture was wholly on the cards and frequently all to the good. The various isms that had plagued our creative and critical writing—impressionism with its vagueness, naturalism with its crudeness, liberalism with its fuzziness, journalism itself, so often shallow and topical—needed reappraisal and at times, certainly, rejection. At the outset, moreover, the new light-bringers and law-makers—whether Eliot or Leavis, whether Winters or the New Critics—were often creatively gifted, critically cogent, polemically eloquent; and were by no means all alike. Where they were most alike was in exhibiting an authoritarian manner and in exercising an academic appeal. And, as time passed, a doctrinal separation of art from life dramatized the separation of the campus from the world outside: even the teaching of English centered on students who would teach it in turn. In the same way, knowledge of society derived from statistical studies, and surveys and questionnaires; the height of a man's brow became as decisive as, elsewhere, the color of his skin; every book or writer served as a measuring rod for praise or a birch rod for punishment. By now men like Mr. R. W. Stallman were not content that art need not derive from experience: they would pontificate that it *must* not. And if it should happen to—well, another such critic decreed that to understand Milton's sonnet on his blindness it was altogether unnecessary to know that he was blind.

What had happened was more than that a too-indulgent journalistic approach had turned into a too-exacting academic one; for that, allowing for enough swings of the pendulum, could have come to a balanced rest. But attitudes, rather than toughening, had petrified. Things became culturally all spotted and pure, saved and damned, and with an actual doctrine of predestination about them. For the wrong people could do nothing right: their new work was prejudged by their old. Hence, what might have begun as an assault on eclecticism wound up as a demand for exclusion; or what began as sound knowledge that there can be no "democracy" in art wound up with almost the feeling that there need be no humanity either.

I have stressed this attitude where it is most fanatical and has doubtless been most often observed. But that it is so intense in limited areas matters far less than that it is so infectious in larger ones. The sleaziness of a success-worshipping culture has created a too-squeamish revulsion. The pander in the one society has begotten the prig in the other; slapped backs have inspired pursed lips; want of integrity has fostered self-righteousness. There has ensued a kind of variant of Gresham's Law, one in which bad money stains and tarnishes good, in which bad taste makes good taste too pleased with itself, in which corrupt standards make sound ones too intolerant. Once again the baby has been thrown out with the bath water, this time for a special reason—because those involved paid no attention to the baby, so concerned were they with saving the soap. Something that stood for humanity, something organic, alive, and capable of growth, was ignored for something inanimate but *pure*.

Furthermore, the constricted attitude breeds displays of the tight puristic mind—bickering, hair-splitting, gratutitous sideswipes. All this might be exhilarating had it any of the lustiness of old-fashioned warfare, any of the dexterity of the true masters of abuse. But it oftenest suggests schoolgirls' hair-pulling matches; it constantly means squabbling that is both solemn and shrill. Or it consist of firing at flyspecks. As a small example, I find a cultivated critic, in a leading Review, taxing a talented writer with a misspelled name. Surely this is sheer proofreader's piddlingness—for which it's the proofreader, if any one, who should be taken to task. In any case, since when has a man's spelling figured in an appraisal of his work? (All the less, I should think, since a man's writing no longer seems to: in constricted circles there are critics of high repute who are quite often scarcely intelligible.) Such lack of charity—which is equally a lack of proportion—is becoming frequent. And about such performances there is much more of Madison Avenue than of Trinity or Magdalen; of victory by fair means or foul than of elegantly caustic wit. English academic castigation can be as amusing as it is deft; America's— as Puritan as it it ponderous—far from arousing laughter, stifles it.

A more central aspect of the constricted life does stem from something genuinely superior in it—from its possession of fine sensibilities. Here, always, the danger must be an ultimate want of balance. In the best-harmonized personalities, and certainly in most first-rate critical minds, sensibility is merged with toughness, delicate perception with solid good sense. Otherwise, beyond an incapacity for seeing life whole, a certain squeamishness must disbar one from experiencing it robustly. One becomes, not at all another Henry James, but a kind of Henry James character. It is not just that the squeamishness usually endows the constricted man with a distaste for the rowdy and lowdown; worse, it means outlawing human emotion and sentiment by dubbing them sentimental and crude. In all this there can be more than something lacking; there can be something dead, or askew. For sensibility comes to exist at the cost of feeling, rectitude at the cost of generosity. People who lack a coarse streak, I have discovered, almost always possess a cruel one. The constricted life, by disliking and dispensing with fists, comes to have fangs.

However repugnant we may find the prevailing vulgarized culture of our time, we cannot, in rejecting it, reject the whole human scene it comes out of. Nor can we assent to the repressive legislation that Constriction enacts: it proceeds beyond guilt-by-association to a kind of guilt-by-non-association-with-itself. There is a sense in which all those not fellow club-members are rank outsiders. There are the right novelists and poets as there were once the right families; and the right magazines, like the right schools; and the right highbrow jargon like the right upper-class slang; and the same lip-smacking scandal over some one's latest article as over a matron's liaison. One can feel pretty sure, in view of his faults and even of some of his virtues, that were, say, Dickens writing now, he would be dismissed out of hand by half the club members who honor his memory. On the whole, however, I am more amused by how they glide over the faults of the right people than by how they demolish the claims of the wrong ones.

I have mentioned elsewhere the girl student at Cambridge University who, when asked by her tutor whether she had enjoyed a certain book, answered: "I don't read to enjoy, I read to evaluate." What is so awful about her remark is that it speaks, not for a single monstrous prig, but for a kind of entire generation. And along with those who read to evaluate can be lumped those who do so only to excavate—to discover new "sources," adduce new analogies, assemble new prototypes. And this is a side of constriction that can catch young people unawares, the side best called Specialization. The victims learn too late that they have made their bed of Procrustes and must lie in it.

The salient point about much of this is the frequent pity of it—how, time and again, good minds that to bear fruit need only light and air, are shut off from them; or how one cultural extreme helps foster another. That sense of extremes—as against contaminating participation, prissy withdrawal—is very marked in our cultural life, so that a quantitative evil breeds its dissenting qualitative one. Still, I am not at all sure that what is contaminating in our culture is always the chief reason for the constricted attitude; I think it is more likely just the pretext or excuse. The basis of priggishness is not what calls for condemnation, but the wish to condemn; the basis of snobbishness is not what calls for exclusion, but the need to exclude.

In any case, our two extremes are helping to leave our culture trapped in a tunnel with no daylight visible at either end. We possess much real high culture, but it suffers, surely, from its self-appointed, self-anointed high priests. Fortunately a critical approach still exists that mates sense with sensibility. Openminded, individualist, humanist, it may sometimes lose its way, but it walks by itself or with a friend, it does not go forth grandly on horseback—followed by foot-soldiers in squad formation—toward walled towns and sacred tombs. Edmund Wilson has become our living symbol of it; but W. H. Auden, Lionel Trilling, Alfred Kazin, Irving Howe —to name just a diversified few—all speak unequivocally for literature, but for literature not sealed off from life. Well, rarely do the excluders wind up unexcluded themselves; nor is it by chance that the literary criticism that has lasted comes from critics who were creative as well (the list is too famous to need quoting) or who wrote in other fields (from Aristotle to Bagehot and Santayana.) The doors of culture must be kept open, no matter what the street noises and smells, or how many odd-looking strangers may, unbidden, walk in. In their own day, for that matter, some of Constriction's mightiest heroes were looked at decidedly askance—when they happened to be noticed at all.

◈◈◈◈◈◈◈◈◈◈

A Taste of Money

LITTLE IN OUR TIME has been oftener quoted than Shaw's retort on Mr. Samuel Goldwyn when, in the course of their negotiations, the businessman stressed art and the artist, money. As a rebuke to the cant men use to disguise their venality, it was altogether fitting; but perhaps its deeper interest lay in Shaw's being as distinctly truthful as Mr. Goldwyn might seem disingenuous. I am also not sure that Shaw didn't know more about money than Mr. Goldwyn; or that he didn't care more. In any case, Shaw's steady insistence, as a great and very famous writer, on his due—his refusal to bate a sixpence from his royalties, or cut a line out of his plays—set a monumental example which has doubtless fortified many writers since. Nor is it odd that it was Shaw who did it, for it was largely what was odd in Shaw that made him. He wanted money for no usual reasons. During his most affluent years, he had a rich wife and no children; did not drink, smoke, gamble, eat meat, have sex or live grandly. He wanted money for prideful or ironic reasons. Certainly it could help heal the hurts inflicted by his shabby-genteel background and his early London struggles. As a puritan again, Shaw—rather like the Quakers—found in money-making his prime worldly satisfaction. As a writer, it somehow gratified him to be a better businessman than the businessman. As a Socialist, it might amuse him to be a shrewder capitalist than the capitalist.

In any case, he remained our century's great example of a distinguished writer who made a large fortune—and by being as intransigent about his principles as about his payments. And yet, if it rejoiced the puritan in Shaw, it just a little jolts the puritan in us. Shaw, on money, got to be a trifle too insistent: however condign the rebuke to Mr. Goldwyn, it too much reassured all Mr. Goldwyn's scribbling minions. The minions might not live like Shaw—without meat, or cigars, or the rest—and might not write like him, either; but it helped them to know that in one very important respect they and he had something in common.

Untempted by the world's fleshpots, Shaw was also unmoved by its glitter. This was rarer than it may seem. In spite of the valid identification of artists with Bohemia, the two real truths in bohemianism are the artist's loathing of bourgeois morality and his frequent lack of good sense about money. But he is bohemian, not ascetic; dislikes Suburbia far more than society; is anti-Wall Street, not anti-wealth. At times indeed he can acquire very luxurious tastes, and be attracted by resplendent and seignorial backgrounds. Snobbery has never been given the serious attention it deserves, if only because few people have viewed it as a serious subject. But in various forms it can go very deep, and it frequently does so with writers. It is too bad that the word *snob* applies today equally to some one over-impressed by his own social position, and to some one over-impressed by other people's; the old distinction of *snob* (the aspiring outsider) and *nob* (the man of position) had real value. More often than we may suspect, the writer is an aspiring outsider. We need only think of the spell that the great world has exerted in all ages on literary men, whether Congreve or Pope, Swift or Sterne, Goethe or Balzac, Henry James or Proust, Scott Fitzgerald or Evelyn Waugh; and again, we need only think why. Being the most imaginative and memory-haunted of men, the writer may, to begin with, be a romantic—in love with a kind of patrician ideal, with a vision of breeding and elegance. His imagination may even make an ass of him; we need only remember, I think in Proust, some one's rapture at being asked to a very grand party and his boredom after he goes to it. And on just those terms imagination, in any perceptive writer, holds open the door while irony enters the room. But the memory-haunted writer may, in a most downright sense, remember slights and snubs that frayed his early life. Or, very simply, the writer could not bear the truth—Meredith, that his father had been in trade; Dickens, that his father had been in prison. Besides, there is even more snobbery about possessing money than about lacking it. By itself money is thought vulgar; it must be chaperoned by something socially acceptable.

And if there is a romantic reason for writers to climb, and a realistic reason as well, there is also a professional one—the interest that many writers have in "manners" and the social scene. Much of this plainly calls for first-hand knowledge. Beyond that, writers can have a desire for money and position thrust upon them —from their being given a taste of luxury that creates an appetite for it.

All these matters vary greatly, of course; and to a large number of writers they do not apply at all. But often one element or another does apply; and even where there is no social aspiration, there can be a cultural or purely economic one. The great point about writers and money today is their unprecedented opportunities for making it. It is all too easy to exaggerate the status of writers *as a whole*—for most of them the economic struggle is still painfully acute, which must be borne in mind with everything that follows. All the same, relatively many writers, often serious and good writers, have the sort of incomes today that a bare generation ago were confined to a handful of great names, or to authors of best-sellers and popular stage hits. In today's age of diversified literary rights, of book-clubs and paperbacks and digests, of serials and syndicates, of dramatizations and movie sales, of permissions and high-paying journalism, of radio, of TV for one's writings and TV for oneself, of lecturing and recordings, of grants and fellowships, of visiting professorships and residencies—an age in which one book can have nine lives and one fee can have six figures—a great many writers, despite high costs and high taxes, can live in the same world, indeed on the same street, as the rich and the prominent.

With this change in situation has come a decided change in attitude. The serious writer needn't think himself a name for the few, or Grub Street an address for the future. Nor need he see, between money and high standards, any necessary clash. Opportunity may not yet have knocked at his door, but it is assumed to know where he lives. Moreover, the moment Opportunity has knocked, all sorts of helpful other people will be writing and phoning and coming to call. Whoever invented the alphabet was clearly writer-conscious, putting the agent *and* the accountant *and* the analyst, at the very beginning. But even with so large a staff— or thanks to it—the writer can prosper. In his progress upward, he will use no executive elevators, and wherever he goes must still be Upper Bohemia. Upper Bohemia may picket Park Avenue; but it must often—by living on both sides of it—have to cross its own picket lines. And its children's schools, as it progresses, become less progressive; its views, as it advances, grow less advanced.

The point of all this is a quite concrete one: that there exist whole clusters of people in the arts who live *expensively*—at times through inherited wealth or moneyed marriages, but oftenest from what they earn. If we look for direct forebears on a *group* basis, we perhaps most readily find them in the Algonquin group of the 1920s. Here were people with citified interests and sophisticated tastes who, by way of Broadway and Hollywood, or of the light-touch writing that came to be centered in *The New Yorker,* made and spent a good deal of money. Witty and worldly, they were moderately concerned with culture and madly competitive about games; if they were lightweights, they effected—*The New Yorker* is the best proof—a kind of lightweight revolution. The most entertaining group of their time, and the deftest at group-promotion, they became in varying degrees the friends, the pets, the court jesters of the unstuffy rich, who wanted to be entertained. Even before the Algonquin set, of course, many individual writers had both the means and the desire to live handsomely: yet even much later, scarcely any other literary circle had an aura of expensive living about it. It is noteworthy how many good writers went to places like Yaddo and the Macdowell Colony; or had guest cottages on rich men's estates; or, if flush, rented a place for the summer; or commonly—which fitted their tastes and their purses alike—contrived to live abroad.

Certainly, during this period, writers had their windfalls and fat years, and accordingly their sprees and splurges. But, even where their bank balances could support stylish living, their anti-bourgeois convictions often protested it. They did not, as so often today, live like rich people, or keep up their end with the rich people they went with. But the salient point is not that till recently writers seldom lived like rich men: it's that they didn't live like businessmen. They had agents to handle their work, and might seek out a "tax man" each year, from sheer ignorance of the tax laws. But few even very successful writers had agents in the sense they do today; indeed, they couldn't have had them in the sense they do today—as operating a vast, complex switchboard plugging in on all the sources of revenue I have already enumerated. And few writers a generation ago could have needed accountants and lawyers in the sense they do today. Today, just how they receive payment, and just when, bulks as large as how much payment they receive. Today, there is a labyrinth of technicalities to thread, of deductions to master; and perhaps such writers' biggest problems today involve real estate and the stock market, trust funds and self-incorporations. Many writers today are businessmen, not in the sense that they personally look after their own finances, but in the sense that they don't—that they employ experts. And the successful writer's day means, exactly like the businessman's, sessions with a secretary, all sorts of business letters and phone calls, an appointment at 10, a conference at 12, a business lunch at one, and very likely a cocktail or dinner date with a business side to it. If all these things on any one day are very unlikely, a day without several of them is even more so.

Thus far I am writing of those at the top. But, numerically, there are a good many writers at the top: if not many in proportion to the whole, far more than there have ever been before, and far faster in soaring upward. But—to move decidedly down—even in a world of notoriously inadequate incomes, the academic world, one finds many and diverse new sources of income. I don't mean salaries, which have generally risen at about the rate of living costs. It is rather how many teachers and professors are now editing textbooks and paperbacks; are now published in well-paying magazines, and appearing on radio and TV; are now lecturing extensively, and winning fellowships and grants. Nor does this apply only to big academic names, or to teachers with outside reputations. The door, now, opens and widens for quite young men, men who are creating a new breed of professor—men who lace their scholarship with sass, who can be at once academic and avant-garde, who go on cultural sight-seeing, and even slumming, tours. One particular field for them is the theatre; in the colleges themselves, "the theatre of the absurd," for example, has won many season bookings. Actually humor, satire, irony, wit appear more and more on the academic menu. Urbanity is not often on it, being still too big a problem for the chef; but the sense of change is noticeable, the degree of change enlivening.

The writer's new status—or, at any rate, new scope—constitutes a genuine gain. Many financial opportunities have opened for the better type of writer, often toward desirable ends. A serious article needs to be written on the pros and cons, the pluses and minuses, of superior writers who currently address large popular audiences in magazines, on TV, on the lecture platform.

Certainly the mass audience is getting far better than its normal fare; and if not many in the audience are converted or even much stirred, that only stresses the glacier-like slowness of solving the problem. In any case, enough good writers today have such audiences as to constitute a kind of working minority. They are not going to win any one over from Yerby's level to Yeats's; indeed, their real value may lie less in making cultural recruits than in halting cultural deserters. A great American misfortune is the disintegration of the college graduate in the twenty years after he graduates—his loss of interest in what he had become acquainted with, his lack of interest in anything since. It is just such back-sliding readers (who have defaulted to the "wrong" magazines) that, by way of the finer voices in them, might be reclaimed.

In contributing to mass media, the writer himself may often have to simplify, but he need not falsify, and need sometimes not change a comma. To be sure, there may be a more than merely ironic disadvantage involved. The good writer's fringe benefits may be turning into his real financial stake, so that the poet makes money largely off permissions; the playwright counts most on that worst kind of audience, the "benefit" audience; the novelist most prospers on a hack stage version or film version of his novel. And if the tail, beyond wagging the dog, is making rather a lap-dog of it to boot, that in itself is no threat to the writer's *creative* career; it can possibly be the one way to ensure it. And certain fringe benefits are, for author and culture alike, true benefits—the serious paperback readers, the university lectures, the poetry readings and recordings at a high level.

The writer's changing financial status necessarily means a change in his psychology. One of the great cultural phenomena of our time is what the sociologist will eventually find a jargon phrase for, but what quite simply can be called the luxury hand-out. I mean all the forms of expense-account high living that many people earlier enjoyed only vicariously, via magazines and movies. Today even quite unimportant writers frequently share in them, and at a high level. The entertainment of fairly unimportant businessmen, however expensive, has seldom much style to it: it runs to the flashier "name" restaurants; to hit musicals, prize fights, World Series games, bars and night clubs. But, for the not very notable writer—who may well be a professor —magazine and publishing-house hospitality often means elegant restaurants, distinguished clubs, dinner with far better known people, besides literary lunch and cocktail parties. The same writer's lecturing involves luxury hotels and rich men's homes. All this becomes part of his professional life, and thus a conditioning factor of his own life. Moreover, along with the luxury hand-out, there now goes what might be called the swapped milieu. As the less stodgy bourgeois and professional world cultivates an artist-world informality, the artist tends toward more stylish and traditional living. The two groups share a penchant for a sort of *couleur-de-rose* peasant culture; the unstuffy rich eschew butlers and dinner jackets for buffet suppers and itinerant bartenders; the artist world fancies good wines and *cordon bleu* cooking, the very same bartenders and on occasion a caterer.

The fact that the two styles of living have grown largely interchangeable indicates something new for the writer, whether in terms of income or of inclination. Upper Bohemia, in one form or another, is an old tradition—but mostly with cultivated non-artists, with well-to-do people of "background" who want to keep what seems right with their world and slough off what seems oppressive. They want Bohemia's casualness without its messiness, they want traditionalism's wellbred comfort without its gentility. Something like this has also characterized *writers* of "background": one thinks of Bloomsbury or Gramercy Park. Their Upper Bohemias often acquire an academic air, or a snobbish and eventually stuffy one. Moreover, writers in such milieus can get to be rather dangerously lionized, or, even more dangerously, tamed. In general America's writers have lived a more careless life than this, whether from a lack of means, or of roots, or of desire. Certain writers might retain from their early life certain touchstones; but at least till well on in years they wanted something freer and unritualized. Or, if the Left Banks and the Provincetowns and the Majorcas were ritualized in their way, it was an anti-bourgeois way.

What the old bohemianism signified was not just a frequent lack of money but a fundamental unconcern for it. Some of its insouciance toward money may have been rationalization; or a prevailing radicalism; or a self-dramatizing romanticism. And certainly want of money could cause serious dislocations, could ruin lives and overturn careers. But there was yet a pretty deep-seated feeling that the terms of economic success, even the terms of bourgeois security, came too high. It was one thing for the Goldwyns to try to fatten their bank accounts by talking up "art"; that was an old, old dodge. But the artist himself—and beyond any romanticizing—had a recognition of his special role. He might at times be making a virtue of necessity, he might elevate into martyrdom the personal mess he had made of things. But the sense of vocation was not just highflown or self-congratulatory; there went with it an awareness of what it entailed—of the people it differed with, the conventions it quarreled with, the sanctities it defied.

To be sure, plenty of serious and gifted artists wanted to make money, wanted to make a lot of it; and a number of them did. Some, like Trollope, were entirely businesslike in their writing habits. Yet the fundamental attitude was different if only because the existing circumstances were. Opportunities were fewer; no book had nine lives. Moreover, bohemian living was not just a protest against bourgeois standards, it was a way of adjusting to economic ups and downs. Writers' lives were often makeshift and nomadic less from having no roots in a community than from having no stake in it. Owning a house meant sweating over a mortgage; possessions had, for a second home, the pawnshop; and banks were for borrowing money, not saving it.

Writing is the legatee, today, of what, whether or

not it has reformed our culture, has in some sense revolutionized it. In spite (or because) of all the class-vs.-mass distinctions, and all the battles of the brows, a much widened market exists for capable writers.* Such writers can be had simultaneously, at every brow level—can be read in the same month in *Partisan Review, The New Yorker,* and *Look;* can be bought on the same day in a scholarly edition, a paperback abridgement, and a popular Digest; can be heard in the same week at Harvard, at The New School and on David Susskind. "Pop" culture, indeed, is acquiring much of the character of the old pop concerts. Just as, along with Strauss and Suppé, the concerts offered the more accessible works of Mozart and Beethoven, so today radio and TV provide great audiences with morsels, and sometimes tenderized meat, from the classics—and from today's avant garde and "controversial" highbrows. Beyond that, on radio and TV there are all sorts of education and classroom programs; of talks by writers and critics; of poets' readings; † and of plays and music. What percentage of the total audience tune in on such things I don't know; but however small, it is huge compared with any pre-radio or TV audience. What percentage of the programs themselves would pass a cultural Pure-Food-and-Drug Act, I don't know either; but that

* Leonard Schechter, in the *New York Post,* described the symposium atmosphere of the first Patterson-Liston fight, with Budd Schulberg, Ben Hecht, A. J. Liebling, Gerald Kersh, Norman Mailer, and James Baldwin all covering it.

† Many poets today, I imagine, make more money from their readings than from their writings.

they very much benefit living artists financially seems certain.

In that very certainty, there is for the have-not writers as well as the haves, for the beginner as well as the veteran, the sense that, with no taint of corruption, the pot of gold lies very close to hand. And already, in certain domains of art, the rewards are blazingly visible. A dozen years after Madison Avenue became a synonym for the big money in advertising and TV, it could as easily, through its art galleries, have become one for the big money in modern painting. In fact it is in painting and the theatre that the arts have most conspicuously become a business—and the artist a businessman in how he functions, a rich man in how he lives. On a very large small scale, there exists today an Upper Bohemia that in its standard of living is wholly top bracket. Its people have the same town and country places as the leisure class; the same kind of servants, of clothes and food and cars; the same architects and interior decorators, the same accommodations in the same ships and hotels. Nor can they be distinguished from Park Avenue on any basis of "bohemian" morality. Drinking, drug-taking, and every form of sexual freedom are as decided stigmata today of the rich man's world as of the artist's. No artist can any longer claim to be a bohemian or a rebel—or an artist—merely by invoking Priapus or Dionysius.

The theatre decidedly provides what is most comic and corrupting in the way of "creative" success. Part of what is both is inherent, from the theatre's own knack for being flashy and its need of being publicized. But part of it derives from Broadway's get-rich-quickness. The classic symbol of this, a generation ago, was Moss Hart, literally stepping out of his clothes to turn his bare back on his past and embark on a "gold-garter" period that, thirty years later, was simply a vast penthouse one. And the symbol has become something of a pattern. There are, for example, theatre people virtually never seen after dark out of evening clothes. One such, a man who first achieved notice celebrating a humbler side of the garment industry, once hailed me at an opening with "How d'you suppose I just *knew* I shouldn't dress tonight?" When, rather staggered, I said solemnly: "After all, it's a Monday night—and raining at that," "No, no, no," he answered. "We just *knew*—the X's aren't dressed either, and I assure you we didn't consult one another!"

What is peculiarly comic is that the splashiness, and the taking it seriously, seem most marked in Broadway comedy writers. Doubtless they have their own way of joking about it all, of being sure to get it said first. All the same, it is not for them a joke. More interestingly, not one of these elegantly fashionable comedy writers has written, with the faintest show of true elegance, a single drawing-room comedy. Yet all this is but the anecdotal side of a great moneyed activity. The sovereignty of money is partly imposed on the playwright by the cost of the investment; is further imposed by the amount of box-office needed to keep the show alive; is finally imposed by the tactics, the pressures, the crises attending it all. There ensue all the legitimate differences of opinion and conflicts of interest, all the creative jitters and collaborating wrangling. And then, and far worse, the producer's itching palm may urge compromise; and then his whip hand decree it. The playwright, by now, has paid out so much in time and energy, in sleeplessness and exasperation, in controlling his temper and losing it, that creative satisfaction has vanished and the only reward is hard cash. The money, indeed, seems less a form of earnings than of damages.

In a quite different sense, the art world today seems too commercial and insidiously corrupting. To be sure, the art world has long contaminated people who worked in it in the precise sense that it refined them: it has provided a luxury life on rather a lackey basis. The luxury handout that is relatively new to the writers' world stretches back for centuries in the artists'. In every age the fashionable painter has been patronized and made a pet of by the rich, to inhabit a world of feasting and flattery. What, of course, makes the art world unique is the personal ownership of the artist's work. Composers, novelists, playwrights, poets offer their work to the public. But pictures and sculpture belong to individuals and institutions. And those who *sell* pictures and sculpture are often akin to those who sell tiaras and Rolls-Royces; and the art world, for all its cultivation, can have a voice quite as "full of money" as Scott Fitzgerald's Daisy Buchanan. It is a world that must not just allow for rich men's whims but that, like any courtier, must pander to them; and unobtrusively, like any guide or governess, correct their taste; and, like any interior decorator, minister to their pride of ownership and display.

The elegance of the art world's surroundings has tended to veil the frequent crassness of its motives. But the art world today is becoming more and more like the theatre world; today, too, there is less, almost, of the studio about it than of the stock exchange. And along with their Hollywood bidding and pricing, picture sales display a Hollywood garishness. Not only have the big auctions become plushier occasions than the grandest first nights; the sums involved make better "theatre." There is one sure way now in America to make what is artistic popular—the way of high finance. Thus dollars do make highbrows of us all: the sale-value of Gainsborough or Cézanne not only achieves headline prominence, it gains philistine respect. What decidedly helped give culture this new status was the $64,000 Question and all its TV siblings. The public saw culture and knowledge acquiring a big market value; and even after the quizzes were exposed as frauds, the taste they had fostered remained. The public is fascinated when millionaires—or museums—fight over pictures. Surely the museums must know that the gaudy prices they pay will set an unhealthful example. The doubtful wisdom of the Metropolitan paying over $2,000,000 for Rembrandt's *Aristotle Contemplating the Bust of Homer* seemed borne out by the crowds who flocked to see it.

I watched them, and their "Ahs" were chiefly for the price and not the picture: they stood in vulgar awe as before a jeweler's window ablaze with huge diamonds. It was itself a spectacle of sorts, contemplating the public contemplating Aristotle contemplating Homer.

Without going into the artistic merits of Abstract Expressionism, surely the prices it has so quickly come to fetch make clear that involved are not just art lovers of Pollock and De Kooning as they might be of Ruysdael and De Hooch, but stockholders in Pollock and De Kooning as they might be of Pan Am and United Carbide. "Works of art" have great commodity value, are top status symbols. As a result, every one in the Big-Board art world is associated with the rich. And this touches those on the buying side as well as on the selling. Curators, like college presidents, are kept busy raising money and angling for bequests; and are to be found, oftener than college presidents, feeding at rich men's tables and imbibing the fumes of wealth.

I haven't traveled this road of art-and-finance hell-bent on achieving a destination. In itself the road runs through picturesque country, offering much that is new and revealing along the way. But the sense grows on one that it has become a heavily traveled road, and one that does reach a destination. Sensibly starting off, away from the genteel slums and messy bohemias of writers in the past, it yet winds up in exclusive residential subdivisions and a sort of conspicuous wasteland.

The writer's position in all this may not be crucial; but his attitude *toward* his position, it would seem to me, is. Time out of mind, he has been fed high-sounding humbug, has heard that his slender means were not only a blessing, but a source of inspiration to boot. He has heard that what loftily set him apart from other men was his *not* striving for material success. Meanwhile, he whose great mission was to tell the truth had often, for a roof over his head, to curry favor. Well, all that has been exploded. My only wonder is whether, with the routing of the old familiar cant, a sort of reverse cant hasn't come to exist—a writer's cant, this time, in which he becomes his own victim. I have the sense that too often today *any* reservations about the artist's relation to money, any setting of limits to his concern for it, are thought arty, or outmoded, or just a new way to bilk him. I have a sense that it is today considered as much the artist's duty to regard himself as a businessman as it was formerly a businessman's dodge to segregate him as an artist.

This may be too glib an antithesis. But what strikes me as literal truth is that writers, as a whole, have been considerably more altered, and influenced, and infected by the life around them than they have themselves altered or influenced that life. And by writers I mean those with standards and values, those who would ruffle the shortcomings of society, not stroke them; who would protest, not comply. It strikes me that, though such writers don't feed pap to the public, they have begun to swallow the public's pap themselves, and that even as they attack America's materialism, in their own way they are succumbing to it. At any rate, it seems pertinent to determine how much of what they have become is mere surface accommodation to the life around them; how much is understandable adjustment to new forces and pressures; and how much, finally, seems a matter of choice and a subject for anxiety.

Certainly much today in the writer's way of life reflects the helpful side of a highly mechanized society. Whatever his other problems, surely it grows harder—on even a modest income—to suffer all the discomforts of home. Dishwashers prevail; diaper services abound; so do laundromats, and community nursery schools, and sitters, and time-saving appliances, and small summer cottages to be had by the month. All these are distinct benefits, and seldom at odds with a writer's chosen way of life. However varied their backgrounds, most writers, having gone to college, have acquired a similarity of surface behavior. Moreover, many writers today lecture and teach. Life, for most of them, grows what once might have been thought crushingly respectable. The party-going is more decorous; the domestic arrangements are more domestic. Writers' marriages may keep breaking up; but writers remarry today rather than live in sin, and their homes contain somebody's children. The children often go to rather orthodox schools. It all constitutes a much modified bohemia, less the result, I think, of changed ideas than of changing incomes.

Much of this is a matter of surfaces. But if writers

conform more, in the sense that they placard their roles less, that is because their roles today gain general respect, and because their economic positions and professional prestige as often soothe their vanity as assault it. Where fundamentals are concerned, most writers worth their salt still live and think on their own terms. Writers haven't had their mouths stopped; and society, perhaps more than ever, is having its nose punched. What seems to me a danger has less to do with middle-classness than with materialism. Still untouched by the old shibboleths, writers are not nearly so immune to the new status symbols. Indeed, the danger may well lie in the actual by-passing of the kind of middle-class standard of living toward which all professional people move —by-passing it for the high-income scale of living which many writers already maintain.

They may still be relatively few, but they bulk large enough to provide an incentive. Moreover, they don't live expensively, in the gambler-style way that artists once did from hitting the jackpot; they do so with every assumption of permanence. Hence certain new factors have entered in. To begin with, when one lives expensively one starts going with others who do, and something embarrassed or self-conscious arises toward writers less affluent. As for the others who live expensively, they can be of many kinds—blueblooded country neighbors, or lion-hunters in town, or executives met on luxury liners. Mixing with them can be both instructive and enjoyable, but it can also foster dangerous identifications. The real danger is that the writer nowadays *can* often truly identify; and can, as seldom in the past, keep financially in step. Nowadays too, as seldom in the past, he may not be much out of step politically. There are few "dangerous radicals" in today's world of letters, while in its social world there are more and more liberals of a sort. A writer's morality may continue sound; but, rather than combat the world, it must often have to skirmish with his own way of life.

An ironical factor in his new approach to living is quite literally the business of the wife and kiddies. It need not even mean a very conservative or conventional wife; she may just be feminine and elegant. At any rate, it is usually she who enforces a more affluent standard once it is reached. Seldom is any of this blueprinted: it just works out that way. But to live so high the respectable writer must often work too hard—the more so, from refusing to prostitute himself. Or, simply from being frequently approached, he will take on too many assignments. And half-smudged creative work born of being too much in demand can prove as harmful as hackwork born of being too little. And what is dangerous, is that each material temptation involves no artistic misconduct, no conscious backsliding. But, after ten years, just where will it leave him?

Not too badly off, perhaps. At the end of ten years, he will still not be stuffy, or Babbitty, or reactionary. He will still eat and drink, and get up and go to bed, exactly as he pleases. He will hate bores, and not be one. He will be unintimidated by fashions in architecture or art or letters; make his own discoveries, reach his own conclusions; speak up for what he believes in and vote for the better man.

The trouble is that all these virtues which still apply to him will apply equally to thousands of enlightened, self-governing businessmen.

A NOTE ON THE TYPE

❖❖❖❖❖❖❖❖❖

THE TEXT of this book was set on the Linotype in a new face called *Primer,* designed by RU-DOLPH RUZICKA, earlier responsible for the design of Fairfield and Fairfield Medium, Linotype faces whose virtues have for some time now been accorded wide recognition.

The complete range of sizes of Primer was first made available in 1954, although the pilot size of 12 point was ready as early as 1951. The design of the face makes general reference to Linotype Century (long a serviceable type, totally lacking in manner or frills of any kind) but brilliantly corrects the characterless quality of that face.

Typography and binding design by
HERBERT H. JOHNSON